More Books from Professors Morrison and Black

Global Explorers: The Next Generation of Leaders

Sunset in the Land of the Rising Sun: Why Japanese Multinational Corporations Will Struggle in the Global Future

The Global Leadership Challenge

FAILURE TO GLOBALLY LAUNCH:

The Case for Aspiring Market Giants

ALLEN J. MORRISON, PH.D.
Kristian Gerhard Jebsen Chair Of Responsible Leadership
And Director Of IMD Global CEO Center

AND

J. STEWART BLACK, PH.D.
Professor of Global Leadership and Strategy

Global Leadership Press
Durango, Colorado

GLP GLOBAL
LEADERSHIP
PRESS

© Global Leadership Institute, 2014
www.globalleadershipinstitute.net

Published in the United States of America by:
Global Leadership Press
559 Miramonte Dr.
Hesperus CO 81326

ISBN: 0615941737

Printed in the United States of America on acid-free paper.

CONTENTS

INTRODUCTION	1
SHOTS FIRED	4
THE GAUNTLET	7
A STORIED START	10
BACK TO REALITY	16
INTERVENTION	21
SUCCESS PLANTS THE SEEDS OF FAILURE	23
READY TO LISTEN	25
APPROACH TO GLOBALIZATION	27
AFG AND THE SNACK FOOD WAY	30
THE SNACK FOODS BUSINESS	31
FROM UCLA TO SNACK FOODS STAR	33
MY FIRST ACCOUNT	34
A STAR IS BORN	34
DINNER WITH AN OLD FRIEND	36
SNACK FOODS INTERNATIONAL?	38
THE TASK FORCE GETS TO WORK	40
A DEPARTMENT IS BORN	42
A SLOW START	43
THE WAY	44

AFG'S ROAD TO EUROPE   47

    THE EXPANSION BEGINS   48

    THE HOME FRONT   49

EXPATS ON PARADE   51

    MEETING THE CHALLENGES   52

BE CAREFUL WHAT YOU WISH FOR   54

NEW JOB, OLD PERSPECTIVE   56

BIG PLANS, HARSH REALITIES   58

    PLAN APPROVED   59

HITTING THE BRICK WALL   60

ONWARD AND UPWARD   62

AN ERA OF NEW LEADERSHIP   64

    STAFFING ISSUES   65

    A NEW GM FOR EUROPE   65

TIGHTENING THE SCREWS   67

    DEALING WITH POLITICS   68

    LOCAL INITIATIVES   68

    MORE REPLACEMENTS   69

LOCALIZATION AND LEADERS   70

THE DEEP STRUGGLE   73

    IT'S A MATTER OF TRUST   77

QUIET INSURRECTION   79

    BRING IN THE CONSULTANTS   80

    THE ACCOUNTANTS' FINAL REPORT   82

    THE REPORT TO THE CEO   82

    THE CEO'S RESPONSE   83

GLOBALIZATION 2.0   85

    THE PLAN   86

    LESSONS FROM KOREA   87

    A FUTILE DEFENSE   88

    OTHER REBELS AT PLAY   89

    MORE DEPARTURES   90

    BRINGING IN THE AMERICANS   91

HIT BY CRISIS 92

    REVENUE WEAKNESS 93

IT'S A MATTER OF BALANCE 94

A NEW "FORMULATION" 96

    THE EXAMPLE OF JAPANESE COMPANIES 96

    THREE LESSONS FROM OUR STUDIES 97

NURTURING GLOBAL LEADERS 100

JOINT VENTURES AND MERGERS AND ACQUISITIONS ... 105

    INTERNATIONAL JOINT VENTURES 106

    INTERNATIONAL M&AS 107

BURSTING BUBBLES AND BUILDING HOUSES 110

ACTION PLAN 114

CHANGING THE ORGANIZATIONAL STRUCTURE 117

FIXING MY TEAM 120

ADAPTING THE CULTURE 122

CAPABILITIES 124

RENEWING MYSELF 127

MEETING WITH THE BOARD 129

BORA BORA 134

    THE COMPANY'S GLOBAL WAY 136

    STAGE 2: DOMESTIC & EXPORTING 137

    STAGE 3: INTERNATIONAL FOCUS 138

    STAGE 4: LOCALIZATION FOCUS 139

    STAGE 5: GLOBAL FOCUS 140

    PATHS FORWARD 141

THE PEOPLE SIDE 143

    INTERNATIONAL DABBLERS 145

    CROSS-CULTURE MANAGER 146

    GLOBAL LEADERS. 147

CIRCUMVENTING THE GLOBAL FAILURE TO LAUNCH ... 149

    THE GLOBAL WAY 151

ENDNOTES 153

ABOUT THE AUTHORS 154

FAILURE TO GLOBALLY LAUNCH

INTRODUCTION

FROM BANGALORE TO BOSTON, THERE IS LITTLE DOUBT THAT COMPANIES ARE confronting tough new international competitors. They may wage battle in their home markets against foreign rivals, or struggle to prosper overseas through exports, or set up shop in some faraway locale. Even the local fruit and vegetable vendor can't escape the clutches of globalization. Frosts in Brazil, strikes in Mexico, and exchange rate fluctuations among dozens of countries from which he sources his produce impact him. It has become impossible to hide from the forces of globalization.

In some ways, there is nothing new to this fight. International business has been with us since before the camel caravans traversed the Middle East millennia ago. But, two things are different for today's companies large and small. First, whereas businesses involved and affected by international business were the exception a thousand years ago, they are the rule today. The percentage of business involved in international interactions has tripled in the last 30 years. Second, over those same three decades, many more organizations have evolved from simple trading shops to complex multinational organizations sourcing, manufacturing, and selling products and services around the world.

Many firms follow a similar growth pattern as they become more international. Most firms start their lives focusing at home. Assuming that goes well, they then expand their horizons by exporting abroad, exploiting what they have done well at home. If exporting goes well, they typically start to make direct investments in foreign markets by building up sourcing, sales, manufacturing, and even R&D capabilities. They do this so their products and services can better fit the needs of different markets. This usually involves sending expatriates from the home country and home office abroad to look after those investments. Gradually, many firms start to hire local managers and often adapt their management practices, as well as their products and services, to better fit local needs and penetrate deeper into the market. Over time, all of this localization can create a confusing and expensive labyrinth of different IT platforms, financial systems, and quality assurance procedures. At this point, firms face the challenge of figuring out what to globally integrate and what to locally adapt.

Our research reveals that many firms fail do not move smoothly along the globalization path and are stymied in their efforts to reach an effective constellation of globally integrated and locally responsive activities and structures. As a consequence, executives often conclude that their companies' decades of investment in globalization have not paid off as handsomely as expected. Going back or giving up is not a viable option. Getting globalization right has become the single biggest challenge many business leaders face.

During a recent executive training program we ran, we discussed the challenges of globalization with a group of leaders from several dozen different companies. After the session, the CEO of one of the largest transportation companies in Asia pulled us aside for a frank conversation. His comments spoke to the heart of his company's globalization challenge. "Globalizing companies isn't really that tough," he said. "The strategic imperative for our company is clear. The tough part is globalizing my people. If we could figure out how to globalize the top management in our company, we would dominate the industry, both at home and abroad."

We have heard similar refrains from many of the managers with whom we work. While the people part might be the toughest, you can't get the people part right without also getting the organization right. The two go hand-in-hand. People and the organization are inseparable. One leads and the other follows—until the order suddenly reverses.

Failure to Globally Launch demonstrates how companies can globalize their operations and globalize their people. Without addressing the operations part of the equation, there is no imperative to address the people part. And, without addressing the people part, all the efforts in the world to globalize operations will no doubt fail.

The principles outlined in this book were derived from over 40 years of combined experience, including work with more than 50,000 executives from virtually every major company around the world. As professors who work exclusively with senior executives from a wide range of industries struggling to meet the globalization challenge, we have seen first-hand what works and what doesn't work. *Failure to Globally Launch* draws on numerous databases and hundreds of interviews we have conducted.

Our research has taught us that globalization is no easy nut to crack. It is complex and affects companies and leaders differently. Communicating this complexity and helping people develop better judgment are also difficult. While diagrams with boxes and arrows or 2 by 2 matrices can be helpful, we have found in executive classroom settings that stories and case studies are often the best way to bring complex subjects to life.

Failure to Globally Launch traces the case of a food company and one of its key leaders as it moves along this path of globalization and the steps and missteps in that journey. We chose to base the book on a company that business readers could easily understand, so the focus can be on the issues and challenges of globalization and not on the intricacies of a particular industry.

Our central story is a real yet fictionalized case, based on true characters and real issues. By focusing on real-world application, we believe readers will be able to relate to the pressures and realities leaders face as they balance career and family—both with what is known and also with what is unknown or even unknowable.

To help readers learn the most from the story, we offer a framework at the outset and then highlight lessons as we move along, especially the common pitfalls that often cause firms to get off the launching pad toward globalization, fail to reach global orbit, and come crashing back to earth.

If this book has one message for business leaders, it is that getting the bricks and mortar of globalization right is not enough. Without addressing the people challenges, including skills, values, beliefs, jealousies and politics, true globalization will come to a crunching halt. This is too often the norm of well-intentioned companies today. Hard work, good intentions, and even smart strategy are not enough. *Failure to Globally Launch* not only points out the common pitfalls and causes, but also lays out a path for success.

CHAPTER

1

SHOTS FIRED

Face a firing squad or face American Food Group's CEO Ron Walker and the board of directors gathered in the 14th floor boardroom at headquarters in St. Louis?

Tie me up and give me a blindfold.

As president of AFG's multi-billion-dollar Snack Foods Division, I'd been summoned to explain why our foreign subsidiaries had fallen behind our competitors in sales and market share—*far behind*. Sales were going nowhere. Not only that, but the board was hearing rumors that we were losing a lot of our foreign managers to rivals and that morale across our overseas subsidiaries was in free-fall. With less than a week to prepare, I put together some thoughts and cobbled together a PowerPoint presentation.

On the day of my presentation, I waited in the lobby outside the boardroom for what seemed like years. My presentation had been pre-loaded on the boardroom computer. I was finally called in and, after a bit of small talk, started with my slides. I acknowledged that we were going through a bit of a rough patch, but I reaffirmed that I was confident that we had a bright future. I went on to explain that we had fallen behind because of the slow progress on our manufacturing rationalization efforts, the slow roll-out of our new IT systems with technical challenges of dropping legacy systems, and the slow capture of anticipated cost savings as a result of such hurdles.

The key word was *slow*. I think I said it seventeen times in the first five minutes.

I turned away from the screen to face my accusers. I'd known Ron Walker since I met him on my first day of work more than thirty years before. He lowered his eyebrows and gave me a curt nod. Not buying it.

I scrambled to add another excuse. "And country manager morale is unusually low." I didn't want to explain why it was low. My real opinion was that many of these managers were lazy and incompetent, but I couldn't come out and *say* that. I'd hired most of them. I turned to look back at the computer monitor that separated me from the board members. "Couple these factors with some regulatory challenges and the lackluster economy—"

An audible sigh interrupted me. I glanced up again and noticed that nobody was looking at me.

Nobody.

I swept the room with my eyes. Not one director made eye contact.

A lump the size of a bowling ball formed in my stomach.

"Is there a question?" The tiny voice was mine, but it seemed distant and disembodied, as though someone else had uttered the words.

Then, like a dawn artillery barrage along the Western Front, the board unleashed a withering battery of questions. Hands slapped the table and fists pounded against open palms. Fingers pointed. Voices rose in volume and rose again. They pelted me with dozens of simultaneous queries.

"Why aren't the cost savings coming online faster?"

"If local managers are dragging their feet, why aren't we holding their feet to the fire?"

"Why weren't the delays caused by foreign government regulations built into our plans?"

"Are we lobbying key government officials to get better cooperation?"

"When can we expect things to improve?"

"Do you have a timeline that reflects when things will change?"

"When can we have the timeline?"

"Nestlé, Kraft, and Frito-Lay are seeing double-digit growth in key markets. What the hell is our problem!? Don't we have the leadership in place to pull this off?"

I couldn't decide which question to answer first. I stood there, motionless and mute. For a moment, it felt as though I were detached, looking down on the whole scene. As I looked, I was amused by the pose I'd adopted—holding one hand in front of me like a traffic cop trying to stem an onslaught of cars. Ron told me later that I appeared perfectly poised under fire. He's a magnificent liar.

I glanced toward the big boardroom window. My nearest escape. I heard the sounds of traffic honking and humming below. The noise of faraway jackhammers and pile drivers from a large construction site pounded in my ears. If I ran at the glass full speed and dove head first at it, would I break the glass and fall to my death or just bounce off the window with only a big bump on my head?

I began to stammer something, until Ron stood and took control of the room. He suggested that I wait outside the boardroom for a few minutes.

I slumped in an armchair in the lobby, staring at the parquet flooring. The bowling ball in my stomach informed me my career was over. I began wondering why I hadn't become a carpenter instead of a marketer. *I* could have been the one who'd built these beautifully inlaid floors instead of peddling crackers and cookies for nearly 30 years, working my way up to these lofty corporate heights only to see my star fall from the sky. I had been instrumental in helping crack the code and get our products exported to Europe. I had been at the center of our effort to build up our operations overseas. We had gone from success to success, and now this?

CHAPTER

2

THE GAUNTLET

WHERE THE HELL WAS RON? I'D BEEN KICKED OUT OF THE MEETING OVER an hour before. How long does it take to fire someone? Were the Grand Inquisitors planning to burn me alive, or would I receive a respectable hanging, followed by the standard press release announcing that David K. Anderson had stepped down as president of the Snack Foods Division for health reasons, to spend more time with his family, or to pursue other interests, including stamp collecting, model ship building, and watching paint dry?

When Ron finally slipped from the boardroom and closed the door behind him, the look on his face was like that of the veterinarian who's about to tell little Suzy that her kitten is sick—very, *very* sick. He pulled an armchair close to mine and sat down.

"How bad *is* it?" I pressed my fingers against my temples hoping to stem the pounding in my head.

"It could have been worse, Dave." Ron rested a hand on my shoulder. "Much worse."

"How much worse?" I dropped my hands and met his gaze.

"You're lucky to have a job. I stuck my neck out for you, reminding the board how you built our overseas presence from scratch. I also told them that you've conquered much bigger challenges before."

I grasped his hand. "Thanks."

Ron squeezed my hand, hard. "Don't be too quick with the thanks." He let go of my hand and got down to business. "I bought you some time.

In two months, the board wants a plan of action with specific detailed lists of deliverables, actions to be taken, deadlines and contingencies if things don't go exactly as planned. Hell, they want contingencies for the contingencies. After that, we'll see."

Two months? How could I come up with a plan that soon? I started to verbalize my protest, "I—"

Ron cut me off with a curt wave of his hand. "They were expecting a solid plan of action in *this* meeting, not a collection of half-baked excuses." He shook his head and lowered his voice. "I expected more from you. You laid a big fat dinosaur egg in there. Not only did you come across as unprepared, you seemed asleep at the wheel."

I slumped back in my chair. "This whole meeting was completely last minute." The stress I'd felt since I'd received the board's summons pulsed on the side of my neck. "I didn't have time to even sift through the data, much less plot a detailed course. It was just last week that I got some real numbers from the accountants and—"

"The board doesn't care." Ron frowned and pounded his fist on his knee for emphasis. "They—don't—care. Listen, I know you've been going through a rough patch lately, what with Sarah leaving."

I didn't reply. The wound was too fresh, too raw.

Ron blustered on with his pep talk. "Before you do anything, take a few days off. Relax, refresh, and come back ready to kick butt, take names, and turn this battleship around. That's all these clowns care about. You *know* that—and you know how to get the job done."

"But I—"

Ron stood and put his hand on my shoulder, his eyes steely. "Just get it done."

"Understood."

"I have faith in you. Always have." Ron turned around and rejoined the board meeting.

I took a deep breath and resumed contemplating the parquet. Then I relented, knowing there was nothing more to do but head home, where nobody would be waiting for me. Nobody to talk to. Nobody with whom I could enjoy a few days off. I wished Ron hadn't mentioned Sarah.

A week earlier Sarah had moved in with her mom, telling friends that her mother needed the extra care, but telling *me* that my career had turned me into a miserable SOB who spent too little time with her and too much time obsessing over crackers and cookies. She even took the dog. He'd yapped at me and nipped my hand the last time I was home.

My career, my *raison d'être*, was supposed to provide my family with material security, not become the instrument of its destruction. Where had I taken a wrong turn? What had I done to deserve this clichéd fate? I didn't want to be another middle-aged executive kicked to the curb during these lean times; someone who'd run a successful company into the ground. Failure wasn't in my DNA. Look how far I'd come at AFG— how much I'd built.

I had enough money socked away to retire, but what was I supposed to do with myself? Make model airplanes until I dropped dead of a heart attack from the fumes of the toxic glue?

The chime of the arriving elevator brought me to my feet. I had serious problems at home and at work. And no idea how to fix them.

CHAPTER

3

A STORIED START

IT'S AMAZING HOW FAST THE COMMUTE IS WHEN THERE IS NO RUSH-HOUR traffic—which is the case when you head home at three in the afternoon. As I paused and waited for the driveway gate to open, I couldn't help but notice how nice our house looked in the afternoon sun, perched atop a small knoll about 200 feet from the gate. The house fit perfectly into the open spot in the woods, but what looked warm and comforting from the outside was cold and empty inside.

I put my keys down as usual in the brass bowl I brought back from Greece several years ago. I walked past the living room and headed toward the family room at the back of the house. I told myself I'd watch some TV and relax. After all, what could I get done tonight given my current state of mind? But true to form, I found myself stepping through the doorway of my study without consciously deciding to divert my intended path to the family room. I sat down at my desk and scanned the walls of built-in walnut shelves filled with a collection of books, awards, photos, and mementoes. My eye caught and fixed on a small memento in the corner, a first-place Little League baseball trophy from 1971. I guess I needed an escape more than I realized, because soon my mind was drifting back to a much more joyful time.

I grew up in the Chicago suburb of Lake Forest, Illinois. My father worked as an accounting supervisor for Greyhound Lines (an amazing bus line in its glory days), while my mom raised my two brothers and me.

My childhood was pretty normal. I played hockey in the winter, and in spring and summer, I played baseball. I joined Little League when I was

10, starting out at third base. By the next season, my strong throwing arm landed me a spot in the pitching rotation. In 1971 at age 11, I pitched a two-hit, no-run game *and* batted in the winning run to take the championship. My teammates hoisted me on their shoulders after the game. It was one of the best summers or maybe even moments of my entire life.

A smile teased at the corners of my mouth while I contemplated the now tarnished prize. Next to the trophy was a picture of me and Jacques Gillard mugging for the camera, with the snowcapped Alps in the background—probably the other great time in my life. It was taken during the summer before a semester of school in Switzerland.

As a high school freshman, I discovered that I had a gift for language. My ninth-grade French teacher told me, "You take to French like a frog to water." (Just kidding. She actually said *fish* to water.) During my junior year, I took part in a student exchange program, spending a month in the summer and then the four months of the fall semester with the Gaillards, a host family in Geneva, Switzerland. Although the Gaillards lived in Switzerland, they were distinctly international. The father was Swiss, the mother was Japanese, and Jacques had travelled on four continents by the time he was a teenager.

My trip to Switzerland was the first time I'd travelled overseas, and my French language skills blossomed. Maybe the locals were being polite, but many of them said my pronunciation was so good they couldn't tell I was an American. Overall, I was surprised that the Swiss and the other Europeans I met were so much like Americans, at least to me they seemed that way. Still, I was struck by a few things. I noticed that many towns and villages were ancient compared with towns in America. It was also a bit odd, at first, to have wine served with almost every meal, and some of the food was a bit different. But after a few weeks, I hardly noticed.

The Gaillards lived outside town in a 17th century chateau, which had once commanded an estate of tenant farms and forests. The stately main house was grand enough to inform visitors that it belonged to a prominent family with old money. The family had aristocratic roots and had been involved in the merchant shipping business for nearly two centuries. They had built a substantial business, first by purchasing ships and warehouses in Le Havre, France, where they still owned a beautiful townhouse. By the 1960s, the Gaillards were importers and wholesale distributors with company headquarters in Geneva but with most of their operations in France.

I spent most of my days with Jacques, who was my age and the only child in his family. He was a lot of fun. Jacques had just returned from spending time with his extended family in Japan and could empathize with my experience of being in a foreign place. He was full of impressive tales and funny experiences, but he also respected many Japanese traditions. His adventures piqued my interest in Asia, and I resolved to someday visit the places he had experienced.

Because of his experiences and multi-cultural background, Jacques liked to think of himself as the black sheep of his extended family, but he was just a normal teenager who loved to have a good time. We got into real trouble only once. We were out for a walk in the center of Geneva on a Saturday afternoon. Outside a drugstore we found a rather large grey French poodle tied to a lamp pole. The dog's owner was inside the store. Now this was no ordinary mutt, but rather the type of poodle you would see at the side of a rich, snooty woman who believed she had royalty in her family tree back hundreds of years. Its coat was spotless white and was perfectly cut and trimmed; it was decked out with ribbons, wearing a pink sweater, and black leggings.

As Jacques and I snickered at its get-up, I decided to try to get the dog to bark. Before we knew it, we had the dog worked into a lather. We were laughing hysterically, when the leash broke and the dog came nipping at us, so we took off running. I was faster than Jacques, and we hadn't gotten a block before the dog clipped Jacques's heel, knocking him to the ground. The dog then started barking at him like a dog possessed just inches from Jacques's face. I was cracking up from across the street, until the dog's owner emerged from the drugstore. She'd heard the commotion, ran out of the store, gave a shriek, and started yelling at both of us. I think Jacques was relieved that someone was finally going to get the stupid dog away from him until he recognized that the dog's owner was an old friend of his mother. By the time we got home, Jacques's mother had heard all about the incident and was furious with Jacques. I didn't have the courage to tell her that I'd started it all. Jacques didn't rat me out; he took all the blame. After that, I knew I could always trust Jacques.

In addition to weekend trips within Switzerland, the family also took me on vacations to France, Holland, and Spain, but I was most impressed with Switzerland. In particular, I was awestruck by the picture-postcard beauty of the villages where I tried skiing for the first time. These hamlets were so pretty and clean that I thought Disney must have built them. During these trips, Jacques and I had a ton of time to talk, both in French and English. He would grill me about life in America: sports, music, movies, pretty much everything.

Tourists sometimes complain that Europeans are anti-American, but I never found that to be true, at least not back then. Jacques thought Americans walked on water. He was always saying that in America, anyone could become a millionaire, even if he didn't go to the right school (he was always worried about getting into the *right* school). He also admired Americans' can-do attitude and complained that Europeans were handicapped by their intrusive governments. Several other Swiss I met said the same thing about their country as well. They complained bitterly about the rules and regulations governing what they could and couldn't do.

One woman talked my ear off about trash disposal. I tried to sympathize, but one of the things that impressed me about Switzerland was how clean the place was. I mean there was absolutely *zero* litter anywhere— not even a stray gum wrapper. You'd think that elves snuck out of their workshops every night to vacuum the country. In the U.S., litter was only beginning to be recognized as a big problem. Back then, too many Americans thought nothing of leaving their trash all over beaches and parks.

I remember thinking Americans could use a little Swiss-style regulation.

Jacques was also a fan of Hollywood films. He loved Clint Eastwood so much that he would dangle a cheroot from his lips (when his parents weren't around) in imitation of the "man with no name."

Though she was as Swiss as could be, the only person who seemed genuinely foreign to me was Jacques's grandmother, Madame Claire. On Sunday afternoons, I often volunteered to help in the kitchen while she prepared the afternoon meal. She had a habit of delivering lectures to me that seemed somewhat narrow-minded and parochial. Though her family's business included importing food products from around the world, Madame Claire refused to use anything but Swiss ingredients in her cooking, preferably local ingredients. For example, she made a point of telling me that the salt she used was Swiss, mined in the next canton. I couldn't taste any difference, but she insisted it was superior. I had similar doubts when she made a big deal of her Swiss sugar. I only knew of sugar coming from sugar cane and as far as I knew sugar cane grew only in tropical places. She quickly corrected my ignorance and pointed out that Swiss sugar was superior because it came from sugar beets grown in Swiss soil that was unpolluted like the sugar cane fields of tropical countries. She extolled the virtues of Swiss wine. I told her I only ever heard that French wines were supposed to be great. She quickly corrected me and instructed me that Swiss wines were so good that the Swiss exported only about 2 percent of their large annual production, because they consumed the rest. As a consequence, she said, the inferior French, let alone Spanish, wines would never touch her lips. Swiss cream and butter were clearly superior, regardless of what the idiot Irish said. And let's not even mention Swiss cheeses.

She was a walking-talking index of prejudices and stereotypes.

Believe me, you did *not* want to get her started on Americans. As far as she was concerned, we dined on cardboard and plastic and watched movies about cowboys killing Indians or about how we single-handedly beat the Nazis.

She wasn't a bad person. She was just eccentric and opinionated. She was like the New Englander who insists that clam chowder rules the culinary universe, or the Texan who thinks nobody else knows how to barbecue. Some people just *had* to convince themselves that *their* way was the right and only way.

Madame Claire notwithstanding, I was addicted to international travel by the time I returned home. From that time forward, I couldn't imagine a career without some kind of international job responsibilities.

After high school, I enrolled at the University of Illinois in Urbana-Champaign. At first, I considered majoring in math, but after taking two pre-requisite courses, I decided that university-level mathematics was an untamable animal. I considered majoring in French but soon realized finding a job as a French major wouldn't be easy. Then, on the advice of my father, I decided to major in Business Administration.

During my senior year in 1982, a number of companies came to campus looking for the best and brightest. Hoping I might be one of them, I interviewed with four companies and received a job offer from an Indianapolis-based pharmaceutical company. The starting pay was $18,400 per year, which at the time seemed a fortune to me. With no other offers and with school debts to pay, I jumped at the opportunity.

In May of that year, I started work as a management trainee, with an emphasis on marketing. I was told I'd be in the trainee position for twelve to eighteen months. However, I was privately informed that management was, "very impressed with my language skills and international experience," and that the company was considering, "international expansion opportunities," for me. If this happened, I could look forward to an international assignment within two years. Now that would be fun.

With this in mind, I dedicated all my waking hours to proving my worth. By 1983, I graduated early from the trainee program and was appointed Assistant Manager. By 1984, my annual salary had risen to $25,200. I had a nice apartment and had paid off my student loans. To celebrate, I bought my first car, a four-year-old Chevy Impala.

Despite my success, I felt unsettled and anxious about the promised international assignment. A few months later, my boss confided that the company actually had no plans to send me overseas. When I asked why, he said, "Budgets are tight and, besides, you're needed in your current job." I was so disappointed.

I began to consider my options. Many universities were offering MBA degrees, and I applied to five different programs. I was accepted by three schools and chose the Graduate School of Business at the University of California, Los Angeles. I liked the idea of going to UCLA because it had a great reputation as a university, its MBA program had been around since the late '30s, plus the school offered me a 50 percent tuition waiver as a scholarship. UCLA also represented a new adventure for me. I had never been to California and moving to the West Coast was appealing. If I had to beat my brains out at school, why not do it in sunny, fun-filled California?

I mostly enjoyed my MBA studies. While it wasn't always fun, I will say that I thrived. In some classes, 40 percent of the grade was determined by participation, and I was always the first to raise my hand with questions or comments. I also admired many of my classmates, seeing in them the same eagerness to excel and find a purpose.

In my second year at UCLA, I met Sarah. She was a senior in the undergraduate education program, working part-time in the library. I needed help tracking down a book one afternoon, and Sarah came to my rescue. It was love at first sight. At least for me.

Also in my second year of the MBA, I realized that I most enjoyed the marketing courses. I soon became convinced that my future would lie in marketing, preferably international marketing. So when the recruiters descended on UCLA in the spring of '86, I applied for only marketing-related jobs. One in particular struck a chord. It was with the Snack Foods division of American Food Group, a diversified food company based in St. Louis. The company offered a wide range of well-known brands, and I had no doubt they all needed the marketing acumen only I could provide. Another plus was the job was based in the Midwest. By this point, the novelty of Los Angeles was wearing thin, and, because my parents weren't getting any younger, I was eager to move home, or at least closer to home. St. Louis was just a few hours' drive from Lake Forest.

CHAPTER

4

BACK TO REALITY

I HAD NO IDEA WHEN I'D DRIFTED OFF, BUT IT WAS 3:00 AM WHEN I WOKE up, slumped in my chair behind my desk in my home office. It wasn't the first time this had happened, but normally there would have been a light tap on my shoulder much earlier, closer to midnight, telling me it was time to go to bed.

No tap on the shoulder tonight.

And no one waiting upstairs.

The crook in my neck forced me to brave my empty bedroom and cold bed. When the morning sun pierced the bedroom windows, I woke expecting familiar noises, but there was nothing. The house was still empty. I went downstairs to raid the refrigerator. I'd not eaten since lunch the day before. I popped some of AFG's famous frozen waffles into the toaster and called Sarah.

She picked up the phone on the second ring. "How did your meeting go?"

"Fine," I lied. I took a glass down from the cupboard and began filling it with water. "How are things playing at your parents' house?"

Sarah didn't answer for a moment. "Everything's fine." Then an even longer pause. "This wasn't an easy decision, you know."

"What decision?" I took a gulp of water. "You said you needed a break. You know the girls will be back home for a visit next weekend." I set my glass down on the counter and stared out the window at the trees on our wooded lot.

"I know." Her voice wavered.

"And so?"

"I don't know," she said with an emphasis that you know after 31 years is a warning not to press.

I stupidly ignored the warning. "How can you not know?" I raised my voice a notch. "I just don't get this whole thing."

"The fact that you don't get it is a big part of the problem." She sounded defeated.

I swallowed hard and took a deep breath. *Keep it calm.* "Well, then explain to me what's wrong," I said gently. "I'm not a psychic. I can't help with your problems and concerns unless you communicate them. Whatever they are, we can fix them. We'll talk them through and come to some common-sense solutions."

"Dave, I've been telling you what our problems are for *years*." She warmed to her task. "You *know* I'm unhappy. You're on the road three-quarters of the year. You're detached from our family life and me. Since the girls went off to college, things have only gotten worse. Our marriage has deteriorated into a roommate relationship. We split some of the household chores and share the occasional meal together, but you're completely disengaged from our home life."

"That's not—"

"You're so busy obsessing over sales campaigns, demographics, and firing people that you've turned into an absentee husband. I feel like the corporate version of the golf widow. You've mentally checked out of our relationship. The man I knew and loved has been replaced by a miserable business executive, who visits my St. Louis hotel once a month." She laughed bitterly.

I struggled to think of something to say that would reassure her of my feelings toward her. "You know how much I love you," I mumbled. I jumped when my waffles bounced up from the toaster. "But you also know that I made a serious commitment to AFG and Snack Foods. It's how I put food on the table, paid the mortgage off, and put our daughters into Georgetown and Dartmouth. That took more than a nine-to-five, Monday-through-Friday routine. I don't mean to sound clichéd, but money doesn't grow on trees."

"Oh, please. Money was never a priority for me."

I slammed my fist onto the counter. "I've done my best to make time for you and the girls, and maybe I've failed miserably, but I had no choice."

"There are always choices."

I scrambled for something to salve her wounds. "Okay. You're right. You're always right. I'll have a talk with Ron. Once I turn around the current situation, I'm sure he'll cut me some slack, and I'll take some time off. We can take that Mediterranean cruise you've talked about. The Greek Isles, Sicily, Hagia Sophia, the bazaars of Istanbul? Or how about the long-awaited honeymoon to Bora Bora? What do you say?"

"Oh Dave, I don't know." Tears filled her voice. "It may be too late."

I tried to sound sunny and naïve. "It's never too late. I'll grab some brochures from the travel agency this weekend, and we'll start going over our options as soon as you get home. How does that sound?"

"I've gotta go."

"When can I expect you back?"

"I'm sorry." She sniffed. "I just don't know." She hung up.

I left my golden waffles untouched in the toaster and wandered out to my woodshop at the back of the garage.

I spent the rest of the weekend in a somnambulant state, somewhere between consciousness and spaced-out. I don't remember what I did, if anything, until the phone rang on Sunday afternoon as I sat staring at the TV screen. Was I watching football?

I grabbed for the phone, hoping it was Sarah.

It was Ron.

"Dave, the board wants to hear from you in *three weeks,* not two months."

"Wha—"

Ron interrupted me mid-syllable. I didn't even get a whole word of protest in. "I know what you're going to say, and I agree. It's impossible to come up with a fully baked plan in such a short time. That's not what they're looking for. They just want to see that you're on the right path, and they aren't willing to wait eight weeks to see it. They're afraid they won't be impressed with what they see then."

"Great. So what you're telling me is that they don't trust me."

"It's not that they don't trust you, but they have lost some confidence."

"That's supposed to make me feel better?"

"Look, Dave. We've known each other for a long time. Like I said before, your report did not go well, but I still have confidence in you. Take some advice from me. Take a few days off. Clear your head. Come back and map out a pathway forward. You don't need all the answers for the board, but you do need to lay out all the questions you plan to answer, and the rough timeframe. You have to convince the board that you're on the right trajectory and that if they give you another five or six weeks you will have a solid plan in place."

"Okay. I get it."

There was a noticeable pause at the other end. "Dave, I know you. In some ways, I know you better than you know yourself. When we hang up, you are going to go into your office and start pouring over the numbers for the last several quarters. Then you're likely to call a few of your team even though it's Sunday here, and maybe even call a few people in Europe, even though it's late Sunday night there. Don't."

I wanted to protest, but Ron was right. I could tell he had more to say. I kept quiet so he could continue.

He waited a second or two so his last *don't* could vibrate in my ears like a struck bell rings until the sound dissipates. "Let me give you an analogy. You know how when you are about to give a presentation at the annual shareholders' meeting and just before you step up to the podium you take a deep breath to catch your thoughts? That's what you need to do now. You need to step back from this for a few days. Take a deep breath. Then come back, but don't try to answer every question. Just lay out what the critical questions are that you are going to address, which ones you plan to address first and why, and provide some basics about the approach you are going to take to finding the answers to those questions. Trust me. If you do this, you'll be fine."

"Okay, Ron. I hear you."

"Dave, don't just hear me. Listen to me and take my advice."

The sincerity and firmness in his voice shook me, and in that instant I resolved that I would do exactly what he said.

"Ron, sorry. You're right, and I do trust you. I appreciate the advice, and I'm going to follow it."

There were a few more pleasantries, and then we hung up. Despite the promise I'd made, the urge to head straight for my office and do exactly what I said I wouldn't do was overwhelming. I knew frenetic activity would just be a *façade* to put between me and an honest look at why things were in such bad shape.

It was now clear. After fourteen years of steering this battleship of a division toward the promised lands, I was foundering in uncharted waters without a compass. I had reached a creative impasse. I had *no* clear idea why Nabisco and General Mills and the rest of our ancient foes were mopping the floors with us in overseas markets. Neither did anyone else. Sure we had problems—mostly with people. But solving the people problems wouldn't necessarily solve our revenue issues. The two were not that closely linked. Even if they were, the best and brightest at Snack Foods were fresh out of ideas. I was their leader, and all eyes turned to me. In three weeks, I would either be the hero or a zero.

I pulled myself back from getting absorbed in all these thoughts and said to myself, *Deep breath.* I had no idea where I was going to go or what I was going to do, but I knew that it had to be relatively engaging or it wasn't going to do the trick.

Without realizing what I was doing, I found myself in my office about to sit down in my chair. *I am pathetic.* As I forced myself to turn to leave, my eye again caught the photo of Jacques and me. Despite the late hour in Switzerland, I picked up the phone and called. "Jacques? *Bonjour* buddy, it's me, Dave."

"David! How is my favorite master of the universe?"

I sighed. "I think I know how Darth Vader must have felt when the Death Star was blown up." Jacques had never grown out of his *Star Wars* obsession.

"Yes, you are a traitor and a member of the rebel alliance!" he laughed. "Are things really that bad?"

"Worse."

"Tell me."

I summarized my predicaments on both the home and work fronts. While I left out some of the details, I couldn't keep the panic from my voice.

Jacques listened, offering an occasional "ah ha" or "I see." When I finished he said, "You American executives always talk about getting the 'thirty-thousand-foot view' of the situation. But you never do that. What you need to do is get a new perspective on your situation. You need to distance yourself from your headlong rush into the future and objectively see where you are now going versus where you *could* be going."

"What do you propose?" I wound my pen through my fingers.

Jacques spoke with assurance. "I prescribe the view from my vacation chalet near Verbier. In the mornings, we can watch the early sun hit the mountains. In the afternoons, we ski. And in the evenings, we eat and drink until we pass out. I am sure through all this, we'll have plenty of time to talk. What could be better?"

"You're kidding."

"You have something better to do? Of course you do. You have to sit in that big house of yours, watching your blood pressure skyrocket as you fret and worry. Enjoy your heart attack, *mon ami*. I will order flowers for the funeral. Or maybe you would prefer that I buy a can of mixed nuts to toss into your grave? This way, we solve two problems at once. We increase AFG sales and preserve your body with the salt."

I grudgingly laughed.

"You are coming then?" He sounded excited. "Good. I will meet you at the Geneva airport Tuesday morning when you get in. *Adieu.*"

CHAPTER

5

INTERVENTION

"YOU SHOULD COME WORK FOR ME." JACQUES DRAINED A THIRD GLASS OF cognac. We lounged in the living room of his Verbier chalet, flames crackling in the fireplace. Through a big bay window, I watched as twilight bathed the snow-covered mountains in pink and purple shadows.

"Are you serious?"

"Yes, of course. Have you ever known me to make such an offer before? I may seem glib on the surface, but I don't joke about the family business. You would be a valuable asset."

"Thank you. But I wouldn't want to take advantage of our friend—"

"No, no," he interrupted. "I know what you are thinking. This would *not* be a mercy hire, *mon ami*. You underestimate the value of your marketing skills and experience. You would be a key asset to the company."

"I'm surprised you'd say that, considering the current state of Snack Foods."

"The troubles that your firm is facing are not of your making—at least not entirely." He sat up and put down his glass as if he had something important to tell me.

I leaned forward, all ears.

"AFG and Snack Foods' international division are confronting challenges that many multinational corporations are now facing, and many of them are also struggling. David, we have been friends since we were boys. Our companies have been trading partners for many years. I followed the evolution of your overseas operations, as well as your career. Though our family business is not as large as AFG overall, we are now bigger than the

Snack Foods business. We have operations in over 30 countries and revenues approaching $2.6 billion. Yes, we move a lot of food. We have also
thought and learned a lot about globalization, about how we can do things
better and differently. Maybe as a private company we have a few, what we
might call privileges in this regard. One of these is the time to study and
think. Maybe this is where I can help."

"And you would have done things differently?" I stared out the window, not wanting to meet the keen appraisal in his eyes.

"May I speak bluntly?"

I turned to face a new firing squad. "Shoot. That is why I'm here."

"Yes, I would have done *some* things differently. But the differences
would not have been pronounced. At least not until recently. Every organization has its unique culture, values, and approaches, and I do not pretend
that if I had been in your shoes, my decisions would have been radically
different during the 1990s and early 2000s."

"But recently?"

He held up a hand. "Even if I had been able to forecast the future, it is
usually impossible to swim against the tide of conventional wisdom in
one's company without drowning. Most likely, my ideas would have been
rejected and even scorned if I'd said we were doomed without adjusting
our strategies to meet circumstances that were not yet obvious. I would
probably have been sent to some sort of management Siberia where top
executives would not have to listen to my ravings anymore."

"Slow down." I turned to my friend, hoping he knew something that
could help me. "Come back from Siberia. What kinds of crazy ideas are we
talking about?"

CHAPTER

6

SUCCESS PLANTS THE SEEDS OF FAILURE

JACQUES STOOD, CROSSED THE ROOM TO THE WINDOW, AND STARED OUT AT the night. "You think Ron Walker and the board would consider some unconventional ideas and explanations of why things are as they are?" He turned to me.

I nodded. "Why not?"

He shook his head. "They have put you on a course to fail. Not deliberately. You have heard the phrase, 'What got you here won't get you there?'"

I nodded.

"Fine. We usually apply it to people's careers and career progression, but it can also apply to companies. Just as it is hard for individuals to see what drove success to a certain point in their careers will not drive success at the next level, often it is hard for companies to see that what was responsible for success at one stage of development can actually get in the way of success at the next stage."

"Okay."

"You say okay, but now I see Ron and the board using the very same strategies and processes that worked in the past. These are not getting AFG to where they want it to go, and yet they insist on still using them." Jacques paused for effect. "You know what the definition of insanity is, no?"

I shrugged.

"Doing the same thing over and over again and expecting a different result."

"Okay, you're right." I rose and joined him at the window. "I'm sure Ron would be willing to consider some unorthodox ideas, as long as I can support my arguments with sound reasoning and numbers."

"Oh, I have no doubt that AFG's senior executives would *consider* your ideas. They would *consider* them just as the crack addict *considers* getting clean once he understands how dangerous his addiction is. But will they actually take action? *That* is another story."

"You're comparing Ron Walker to a crack addict?" My brow furrowed.

Jacques laughed. "I'm saying that even the best advice is useless if it does not have a good chance of being implemented. The quality of the advice may be obvious to you and me, but old habits and mindsets die hard. Your younger managers, especially the non-Americans on your teams, may see the value of these crazy ideas, but your key decision-makers in the home office are *very* set in their ways. They may interpret your recommendations as dangerous heresy and an affront to the values and business models that have fueled AFG's success for generations."

"How crazy are these ideas? I'm a drowning man, Jacques. Throw me a line."

He turned to me, more serious than I'd ever seen him. "If you present these ideas and really push for them, you will be like a modern-day Martin Luther, nailing your theses to the foreheads of the Pope and his cardinals. It would take a diplomat of the highest order to make AFG execs see the light—unless they are desperate enough to give your notions a trial run."

I laughed. "Desperate? If that's what you need, I can supply a whole company of desperation." I sat down. "Why haven't you ever said anything before? It's unusual to find a man full of ideas who isn't eager to share them."

Jacques shrugged. "It was not my place. You never asked for my advice, so I assumed you would not appreciate it. Besides, I haven't thought that you were ready to hear it."

"I'm sorry. I've been overwhelmed with the globalization mess. I'm ready now, old friend."

"Don't worry." Jacques smiled. "I have taken the liberty of inviting some colleagues to help with our discussion. They will arrive in the morning. When we are finished, we'll have time to ski in the afternoon. You should not be so hard on yourself. AFG is not alone when it comes to these bumps along the overseas road."

"All our competitors seem to be doing great."

"Maybe on the surface, but other multinationals have encountered similar problems when trying to balance their efforts at localization and globalization." He drained his glass. "Let's leave it for tonight. You need to relax as much as you need some insights."

"Fair enough." I was eager to hear Jacques's view of my situation, but instead of tossing and turning half the night, the combination of jetlag and stress hit me, and I slept deeply.

When sunshine and the aroma of fresh coffee roused me the next morning, I realized I had slept much later than usual. The crisp mountain air and Jacquess calm assurances had a good effect on me. I couldn't remember the last time I'd slept so soundly.

His first words, however, jolted me awake. "David, you remember Hans Schroder? He is one of my colleagues who will arrive in one hour."

I rolled my eyes. "Will you supply me with body armor before the meeting?" In a past life Hans had been the GM of Snack Foods in Germany, and I was less than confident that his memory of me was pleasant.

"Only a knife and a canteen." Jacques smirked. "If he doesn't hunt you down in twenty-four hours, you will be allowed to go free."

I slumped in my chair. "I can't wait."

"In all seriousness, he is not bitter over his experiences at AFG." Jacques warmed to his subject. "On the contrary, he and I have been working on a research project to help my firm overcome some of the same challenges that you are now facing. I think you will be fascinated by what we have learned and the initiatives we have developed."

Ready to Listen

By ten o'clock that morning, I was facing Hans Schroder and a well-dressed young woman, Anjanette Bernard, who was vice president of human resources at Jacques's company. Jacques sat at the head of the dining table.

I'd worried that my reunion with Hans would be awkward at best, but the ex-Snack Foods executive greeted me like an old friend as we shook hands, even inquiring about several former colleagues back in St. Louis.

After pastries and a few pleasantries, Jacques cleared his throat. "Now that we are all acquainted or perhaps reacquainted, why don't we brief David on our research findings and new initiatives?"

We moved into the lounge and settled ourselves in overstuffed leather chairs. Hans pointed a remote control at the flat screen TV. A PowerPoint slide bearing Jacques's company's logo lit up.

Jacques began, "Let's start with some perspective. As I said earlier, we have been researching companies all over the world, and we've found that no matter where they began, most follow a similar path as they grow. Before we specifically consider AFG, let's hear what Anjanette and Hans have to say. Then I will summarize where I think your company is today, and how it reached this stage. After that, I'll share my recommendations."

I glanced around the room and grinned. "Can't we just skip ahead to the answers?"

Hans smiled politely, but it was clear he was not going to skip any-thing. "What do Icarus, a 2009 NASA rocket, several dozen Japanese com-panies, and AFG have in common?"

"I have no idea."

"Let me start with the ancient Greek myth of Icarus," he began. "As the myth goes, Icarus and his father, Daedalus, were imprisoned by King Mi-nos on the island of Crete. To escape, Daedalus crafted two pairs of wings out of wax and feathers for himself and his son. Daedalus warned his son not to fly too close to the sun. However, overcome by his success and the fun of flying, Icarus soared high into the sky and came too close to the sun. The sun melted the wax in his wings, and he fell from the sky into the sea, which today bears his name: the Icarian Sea in the Aegean."

"Okay, nice story, but what is the point?" Frustration tinged my voice.

Hans smiled. "Part of the message is that getting too carried away in success—flying higher and higher—can ultimately cause failure."

"So next you are going to tell me about a NASA rocket that flew too close to the sun and melted?" Everyone laughed, but I couldn't imagine how Hans was going to link Icarus to a NASA rocket.

"Not quite. On February 24, 2009, after an initial brilliant liftoff, a $280 million NASA rocket failed to climb high enough to reach global or-bit and crashed back to earth. The rocket carried the highly anticipated Or-biting Carbon Observatory satellite, designed to study the earth's capture of carbon dioxide, and its contribution to global warming. NASA officials said a protective cover on the satellite failed to release and fall away just a few minutes into flight. This small but significant extra weight kept the satellite from reaching orbit."

"Great. So the moral of the two stories is that if I go too high or don't go high enough, I'll come crashing back to earth."

"A bias for action or quick conclusions," Jacques interrupted, "is not always the right thing. Sometimes you have to take a step back and pa-tiently reflect to see clearly."

Hans took his cue and continued. "The point of the NASA rocket story has two parts. Yes, like Icarus sometimes initial success does not guar-antee ultimate success as NASA's successful launch but ultimate failure illustrates. Also, sometimes we have to let go of things we needed at one time, like the protective cover on the satellite for initial launch, in order to go higher later."

"Okay, I'm with you. I see the link between these two, but I think you said the third and fourth things were Japanese multinationals and AFG. I have a hard time imagining how they can link to the first two examples."

Hans asked, "Do you remember when people felt so threatened by Japanese companies back in the 1990s?"

I nodded. Some Japanese company had bought the Rockefeller Center in New York and another had bought the Pebble Beach Golf Resort in Cal-ifornia for astronomical sums. I remember people were petrified Japan would buy up most of America and take over the world.

"What you might not know is that in 1995, *Fortune* published its first

Global 500 ranking. The top three companies were Japanese, as were six of the top ten. A total of 141 Japanese firms were named in the top 500. Together they had more revenue than all the U.S. companies on the list, even though the U.S. economy was about three times bigger than Japan's. Unfortunately, their brilliant liftoff was not followed by a glorious triumph of reaching global orbit. Instead, they came crashing back to earth. By 2010, just fifteen years later, the number of Japanese firms on the list fell from 141 to 68."

"Wait a second," I interjected. "Are you saying AFG has crashed? I know we're struggling in some places, but we're still a great company. Why are you grouping us with them?"

Jacques knew when to soothe my nerves as only an old friend could. "AFG is not in the same position as these companies," he said. "At least not yet. These are the most visible examples of what we are calling the *Failure to Globally Launch Syndrome*. In other words, like Icarus or the NASA rocket, we can achieve initial success, but it can get in the way of future success. You still have a chance to activate the booster engines and make it to global orbit."

Approach to Globalization

Hans continued. "Our study found that companies approach globalization with various tools and strategies at their disposal. Some companies are highly sophisticated in their preparations and complex in their approaches; others pursue a simpler, bare-bones path. Regardless of the approach, companies have only two basic tools for globalization at their disposal. First, they can sell their goods or services overseas by exporting or trading them. Second, companies can sell overseas by investing in foreign countries and producing locally.[1] Investment, or Foreign Direct Investment (FDI), includes money and materials to build factories, distribution centers, warehouses, or other infrastructure.

"While not all companies leave their home markets, those that do tend to follow a common path." Hans clicked the remote and a chart filled the TV screen. "We consider five distinct stages of development, starting with domestic, extending to exporting, then international, localization, and finally borderless globalization" (see figure 6-1 below).

Figure 6-1

Stages on the Path of Globalization

HIGH

STAGE 2 domestic + exports		STAGE 5 global focus

TRADE   STAGE 3
international
focus

| STAGE 1
domestic
focus | | STAGE 4
localization
focus |

LOW

LOW   **FDI**   HIGH

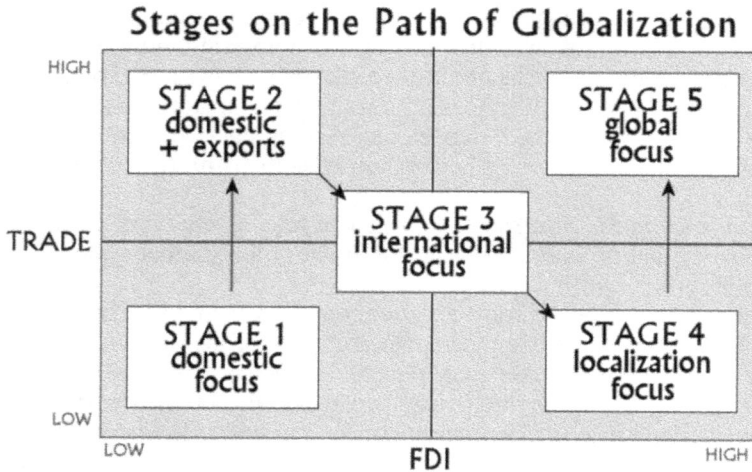

Hans moved to the front of the room and pointed at the lower left square on the screen. "Until recently, it was virtually impossible for a company to be born global. The largest companies today were started thirty, forty, even over a hundred years ago. Virtually every one of them was born in one particular country. For example, General Electric was started in the U.S., Michelin in France, Toyota in Japan. Not only are most companies born in a single country, but they also spend their early years primarily in their birth country."

Anjanette, who had been silent up to that point, spoke up. "Like small children, companies are influenced by the language, culture, customs, and practices that surround them, especially when they are young. In business, the equivalents of influential parents, friends, and neighbors are the business's customers, competitors, employees, suppliers, regulators, and shareholders. These influences have a dramatic impact on the *cultures* of the firms, including their dominant model of effective leadership. The degree to which companies successfully respond to these influences will affect how they subsequently internationalize."

I looked at Jacques and smiled. "Without a doubt, my first trip to Europe when I stayed with your family had a huge impact on me. I never thought about how country culture could impact the culture of companies."

Hans moved our attention back to the slide. "The second stage is about exporting. Companies that are successful at home are often tempted to increase sales through exports. The tougher their home market and the more successful they have been, the greater the attraction of exports and the more likely their exports are to be successful. In addition, for manufactured goods where any economies of scale might apply, it makes sense to use your full production capacity, lower per-unit costs, and increase margins and profits at home. This can all be achieved by capturing additional revenue abroad with exports."

Jacques turned to me. "Think about your first discussions with management about exporting to Europe. Do you think AFG believed their success at home would be easily translated in other markets?"

I responded with a shrug of acknowledgment.

Jacques continued, "Perhaps you begin to see why we grouped Snack Foods with the Japanese firms. You achieved success in your home market and then decided exports could add some additional revenue while also helping to lower unit costs. This is classic—and exactly what helped the Japanese firms grow.

"The expansion had a few hiccups along the way," he added, "but it proceeded smoothly enough to generate confidence—even hubris. Because success breeds complacency, your executives had no reason to change course. AFG is not the only company that followed this path."

Jacques stood up. "I know just what we need right now. Give me two seconds." He left and came quickly back holding a bag of one of AFG's original exports. He was grinning. "You see, you have been very effective in converting me to a Snack Food follower. I love Chocolate Chippers as a midmorning snack."

He offered the bag to Hans, who drew out a cookie and took a bite. "Jacques isn't the only one. I also love these cookies. Sometimes I still wish we had them in the office pantry."

I watched three people—from Switzerland, Germany, and France—enjoying my company's cookies, and my bruised ego felt a little better. To be sure, the principle reason for exporting was to increase sales and profits, but I'd also wanted people from other countries to enjoy the snacks I loved growing up.

Just then the phone rang. Jacques answered and after a few seconds, he covered the phone and told us, "Hey, I have to take this, but this may be a good time for a break anyway. I'll come back in fifteen minutes."

I nodded and waved him to take the call. I did need a break. Something with their company was clearly up, because Hans and Anjanette also reached for their iPhones and began replying to emails and text messages.

I took the opportunity to step outside on the deck and take in the mountain air. Relaxed, my mind started drifting back, considering AFG's origins and where it had come over the years. I thought about the early international years, when AFG had moved into exports, and the progress from its beginnings to where we were now.

CHAPTER

7

AFG AND THE SNACK FOOD WAY

AFG TRACED ITS ROOTS BACK TO JEFFERSON CITY, MISSOURI IN 1845 WHEN James Stanton opened the Liberty Flour Mill, situated on a creek that flowed into the Missouri River. The creek drove the water wheel, and the mill ground wheat and corn for local bakeries and food processors. The mill gradually expanded its customer base to include stores and processors in nearby St. Louis.

In the early 1900s, Liberty expanded its milling and bakery operations and diversified into grain storage, livestock feed, and bakery ingredients. By 1936 Liberty was manufacturing biscuits and crackers, refining spices, and making yeast-based bakery products. To reflect the diversified product lines, Liberty changed its name to American Food Group, and in 1951 the company went public.

In 1986, the year I was hired, the CEO was Brent Miller. AFG by then had 28,700 employees and sales of $479 million. It ranked in the top 200 on the Fortune 500 list of the country's largest companies and was organized into four major divisions:

Agribusiness – which included nutritional products for livestock and branded pet foods.

Bakery Products – including milled flours and baking mixes sold to both consumers and industrial buyers.

Snack Foods – which included cookies, crackers, potato chips, pretzels, and peanuts.

Fresh Bakery – including breads, rolls, buns, and specialty breads. AFG was the third-largest fresh-bakery business in the country.

AFG was well known in St. Louis, where it was the city's fifth-largest employer, and throughout the country. Its brands were stocked in virtually every grocery store in the country and, not surprisingly, AFG was a major advertiser. In the 1970s, its ads for snack foods and cake mixes were regularly seen in Life, TV Guide, and Redbook magazines. In 1974, one of its print ads won a prestigious national advertising award. AFG also advertised on all the major U.S. television networks and ran billboard advertising in major urban areas.

The Snack Foods Business

Snack Foods was AFG's second largest division, right behind Bakery, employing more than 9,500 people. Its headquarters (where I worked) employed 600 people in downtown St. Louis.

Snack Foods occupied two floors of the head office building. Its support facility was five miles away, where the bean counters and scriveners worked. Snack Foods also ran sixteen distribution centers and eleven sales offices in the US, most of which employed between thirty and fifty people.

Snack Foods operated four bakeries in St. Louis, Chicago, Dallas, and Fresno, California. It also had twelve potato chip manufacturing facilities and two peanut roasting plants, one in Georgia and one in Texas.

Snack Foods competed on the basis of its high product quality and strong brands, but it trailed behind Nabisco, Pepperidge Farms, and Frito-Lay in its percentage of revenues spent on new product development. Its wide range of brands had mostly been acquired from small, localized companies during the previous forty years. To sharpen its focus, in 1982 product development was centralized in St. Louis, and a new policy was introduced that discouraged the development of additional local products. A new vice president of product development was hired, and between 1982 and 1986, R&D budgets in Snack Foods increased by 65 percent.

Within Snack Foods, a range of pressures affecting production scale efficiencies, plant and sales office locations, and branding decisions buffeted each product line. For example, crackers were more shelf-stable than cookies, but demand was more seasonal—sales spiked during holidays. By contrast, demand for cookies was much higher and more predictable; cookies were more open to brand extensions than crackers or pretzels were. Potato chip plants offered relatively low-scale efficiencies, leading to the proliferation of local potato chip brands. Through industry consolidation, many of the local brands evolved into regional competitors.

When I first joined AFG its sales included the following (see Figure 7-1):

Figure 7-1

Snack Foods Sales Levels (1986)

	% Of Sales Through National Accounts	% Of Sales Through Regional Accounts	% Of Sales Through Local Accounts
Cookies	31%	42%	27%
Crackers & Pretzels	53%	40%	8%
Potato Chips	8%	50%	42%
Nuts	-	100%	-

Although the numbers were fairly static, it was clear that Snack Foods' ambition was to shift from smaller, more resource-intensive local accounts to larger national brands.

It was only after I started working at Snack Foods that I began to get a feel for the organization's culture. I quickly learned that the employees were particularly proud of the values and common behaviors that united them. The year I started at AFG, an outside study of values shared by Snack Food employees revealed several common employee attributes:

- They were highly competitive.
- They appreciated hard work and were people-friendly; i.e., the employees liked each other and enjoyed socializing together.
- They were informal. People used first names, and it was rare to see an employee (even in sales) wearing a suit and tie.
- They enjoyed a good, boisterous party—the louder the celebration, the better.

Among Snack Foods managers, this culture was known as *The Way*, a variety of related unwritten (and largely unspoken) codes of conduct, expectations, behaviors and values. *The Way* demanded absolute loyalty to Snack Foods and the chain of command, i.e., no ass-kissing and politicking to secure promotions. The bottom line was the *only* yardstick against which performance was measured. Honesty was valued; we said what we meant, and we meant what we said. We were expected to exceed targets without excuses. Most important, we were expected to beat the competition and beat them big time.

Snack Foods had a reputation as a tough division within AFG and was the most selective in its recruitment. Personality "fit" was deemed essential. Once hired, few people ever left Snack Foods, and virtually no one moved to the other AFG divisions. Those who did were regarded as traitors or washouts.

Irrespective of division, AFG worked hard to develop close relationships with its retail and industrial buyers. AFG's eight-step sales process was mandated for all sales employees. Six of the eight steps focused on relationship management to identify, build, maintain, and exploit personal customer ties. Sales reps were required to keep a binder with them listing every customer they served, where customers had gone to school, names of their spouses and children, the type of cars they drove, and even favorite recreational activities. The details were used to tailor sales interactions with customers.

Strong relationships with local buyers served AFG's business divisions quite well. Customer needs varied throughout the country, and close relationships allowed AFG to better provide product and service solutions. For example, baking was more common in New England than in the South. Southern customers tended to favor fried foods. Mexican and organic foods were more popular in the Southwest, while European-based ethnic foods were favored in the East and Midwest. Effectively responding to these needs was critical to AFG's marketing success. No matter what was being sold, listening to customers and responding quickly were values shared throughout the entire AFG organization.

Of AFG's four divisions, Snack Foods was thought of as the place to be if you had real potential as a manager. Sales reps shared a universal drive to one-up their colleagues in other divisions by beating them on sales and earning higher bonuses. To some people, this was a game, but to others it was a life-and-death struggle. Bonuses could amount to as much as 100 percent of base salary; they were publicly posted at headquarters and mailed to every sales office. Any rep who didn't make 90 percent of his sales target over two consecutive years was fired without recourse.

I managed to fit right into the Snack Food division and was pegged early on as a high potential manager. I had a strong competitive drive, and from my initial hire out of UCLA right through my first few years, I seemed to be a natural for the job.

From UCLA to Snack Foods Star

Sarah and I were married in California after I graduated from UCLA, and we moved to St. Louis. I was excited about my first job as an assistant marketing manager in the Cookies Unit. When I was shown to my office on my first day at work, I was surprised that it wasn't an actual office, but a space that consisted of a metal desk with a melamine top, a floor fan, a desk lamp, and a wooden chair that probably dated to World War I. Not exactly what I expected as a newly minted MBA. But hey, we all have to start somewhere.

The Snack Foods Marketing Department shared the fifth floor with the Sales Department. Our mission in marketing was to create end-user/consumer demand largely through promotions. By contrast, the sales department focused on winning over the retailer. Like brothers and sisters, we were sometimes chummy in a those-guys-aren't-so-bad kind of way, but at other times we were at each other's throats. The elevator bank in the middle of the floor was the demarcation line between the departments. Back in '72, the VP of Sales even had the floor tiles replaced on his side of the elevator banks as a way of staking out his territory. The tiles had never been replaced.

All of Snack Foods reported to Ron Walker, the division president. At 45, he was the youngest of AFG's four division presidents. Ron surprised me when I was introduced on my first day of work because he already seemed to know who I was—and I never forgot that.

Five category VPs reported to Ron: cookies, crackers, potato chips, pretzels, and peanuts. The VP of cookies was 57-year-old Stu Rogers; he was a great guy, but most people assumed he would retire in a few years. Within the cookies category, there were seven brand managers. One of these brands was Chocolate Chippers. Its manager was 41-year-old Brad Jones. He'd become a brand manager ten years earlier, and since then had managed four different brands. All of them had been in trouble when Brad was put in charge, but they were in great shape by the time he moved on. Brad was my first boss.

My First Account

I loved my first assignment. Not only did I get to work on a brand that needed a boost, but I also reported to someone with years of experience and a reputation for letting assistant managers who were up to it take on significant responsibilities. Chocolate Chippers was the division's single largest product line, accounting for 50 percent of total cookie sales and nearly 10 percent of divisional sales overall. This was a plum assignment!

Given my MBA marketing knowledge, Brad made me the liaison with the Madison Avenue firm of Ogilvy & Mather, responsible for creating a new Chippers ad campaign. The ads were scheduled to run in seven months on the afternoon soaps like *All My Children* and *One Life to Live*. My job was to tell the folks at Ogilvy what Snack Foods wanted for key messages. I was also charged with ensuring the ads strengthened the brand, deadlines were met, and results exceeded the high standards set by the business.

Although working with Ogilvy was challenging, I persevered. The finished ad reels were delivered on time and only 10 percent over budget. The campaign's launch was a huge success. By summer, sales of Chocolate Chippers were up 10 percent. By the following winter, they were up another 8 percent.

A Star Is Born

My star was rising. I knew I wouldn't remain an assistant marketing manager for long. In June 1987, I was told to drop the "assistant" from my title.

In my next assignment, an entirely new position, I reported to Peter Kent, the head of marketing for all categories of cookies. I was made responsible for every cookie ad that aired during the afternoon TV soaps. In addition to Chocolate Chippers, this included five national cookie products. After surviving the "get acquainted" period with Ogilvy, I retained them as the lead ad agency but also added J. Walter Thompson, a New

York firm that had managed Scotland's Own cookies, a butter-laden short-bread originally limited to New York and now being rolled out nationally.

After a lot of prodding from me, both companies created winning ads. Rather than overwhelming one show with cookie spots, we decided to spread our ads across all the afternoon soaps. Once again, cookie sales rose. I remember bumping into Division President Ron Walker one day, and he told me how pleased he was with my success—and he added that he was proud of his personal role in recruiting me. This was news to me. Good news. Soon I was the talk of the marketing department, and my face beamed every time I walked the halls toward my office space.

Fresh from my success with the afternoon soaps, I got Ogilvy to work up a Chippers ad for kids watching TV after school, and those ads were another huge hit.

From then on, I could just about write my own ticket. At a minimum, I knew my "space" would soon include four walls and a door.

CHAPTER

8

DINNER WITH AN OLD FRIEND

MY SUCCESS DID NOT COME WITHOUT A PRICE.

I was on the road nearly 180 days during 1987. That was tough on Sarah—on both of us.

My old friends from university hassled me, too, about my career choice. Cookies? Soap operas? Cartoons? *Really*? At a UCLA class reunion, a former classmate called me "cookie boy" at dinner, and before long the whole table was chanting, "Cookie boy, cookie boy!"

Even my father-in-law gave me a hard time. "Did you really get an MBA to sell cookies to bored housewives?"

Good question. But I loved my job. Not only did I sell products that people enjoyed, I could measure the results of my efforts.

It was late 1987. After years of infrequent contact with Jacques, he called and said he was going to be in the U.S. and wanted to get together. He would be visiting New York during the Christmas holidays. Despite Sarah's objections to my vagabond lifestyle, I could always find a reason to be in New York, so I arranged to meet Jacques on December 28th.

In typical European fashion, dinner lasted nearly two hours; we had lots of catching up to do. Toward the end of the evening, Jacques dropped a bombshell. He was leaving his current job to take the reins of the Gaillard family business because of his father's ill health and the family's lack of confidence in the current management.

"If you recall," he said, "we are one of the largest grocery products distributors in Switzerland and France. Perhaps you know someone in the food industry? Someone who might be interested in introducing American products to Europe?"

"You jerk." I punched him on the shoulder. "You waited until *now* to mention this?"

"For a corporate suit, your strength is amazing." Jacques rubbed his arm in mock pain. "You must be lifting weights."

I grinned at him. "I'll bench press *you* a few dozen times if you don't give me the details."

"Okay, okay." He held his hands up in surrender. "So maybe I held back this morsel of news just to watch the look of surprise on your face. It was worth the wait." But then he added, "It is getting late. Let's reconvene at breakfast, and I'll go through everything with you."

The next morning, we met at breakfast to discuss AFG's product lines and ways we could push them into Jacques's distribution channel. By mid-morning we had reconvened in his hotel suite, and by afternoon we'd agreed on the products that would make the best debutantes in a half-dozen European markets. Not that I was in a position to speak for AFG, but it just felt so right.

I was especially excited about crackers. As an exchange student, one of my few epicurean disappointments was French cheese and crackers. The cheeses were a tart and creamy delight, but the crackers tasted like compressed raw flour. Dry, bland, and boring. The reason for the cardboard flavor, said the French, was that crackers were not supposed to interfere with the flavor of the cheese. Nonsense. AFG's food scientists knew that butter and the salt content of crackers actually enhanced the flavor of cheese.

Jacques agreed with my reasoning, but strongly recommended that we avoid words such as "science," "formula," and "formulation," when it came to European advertising. Though it would be years before artificial ingredients and genetically engineered farm products became suspect in U.S. markets, most French consumers were already loath to buy foods that smacked of laboratory manipulation. Baked goods promising old-fashioned, stone-ground goodness, on the other hand, were always in demand. We had already adopted this positioning for our Frisco-brand crackers, so no reformulation would be necessary if we focused European sales on this product.

CHAPTER

9

SNACK FOODS INTERNATIONAL?

When I returned to St. Louis, I wasn't sure how to broach the opportunity with my boss. Stu Rogers, VP of Cookies, was born and raised in the Midwest. He'd never ventured much outside the U.S., and I was sure that he would have little or no interest in international opportunities.

As luck would have it, Ron Walker called an all-hands-on-deck meeting just after the New Year. I rarely had a chance to meet with the division president; this was an opportunity too good to pass up. At 10 a.m., most everyone gathered in the corporate auditorium to hear Ron outline his plans for the coming year.

"Last year was a good year for Snack Foods," he began. "Overall, it looks like our sales will show an increase of 3 percent. We are now the fourth largest cookie company in the U.S., and our cookies are number two in St. Louis, Houston, and Denver. Our peanuts and mixed nuts have climbed from number seven in the U.S. to number six. In crackers and pretzels, we're also on the move. I am particularly proud of the progress made on our Twirly Swirly pretzel line, which is now number three in California and number one in San Diego. Potato chips had a tough year. Sales look like they're going to be off by 6 percent overall. We need to do better, particularly in Texas, where sales were down 11 percent.

"In fact, despite the progress we have made as a division, we all need to do better. The market is tough, and we have a lot of strong competitors. We have to grow, and 3 percent just isn't good enough. There are a lot of new expansion opportunities out there and, while the U.S. is our home and our future, I'm charging every business unit with developing new ways to expand our sales—not only in this country but in Europe as well. Europe is a huge market, and we are doing nothing over there.

"The Europeans eat a lot of snack foods," he said. "Our production lines are nowhere near capacity in this country. Let's find ways to sell products in the U.K., France, and Germany. I'm not talking about a major new capital expansion, but I *am* talking about exports!"

Isn't life full of surprises? By the time Ron was done, I was ready to rush the stage and give him a hug. Exporting to Europe through Jacques's company, at least for France and Switzerland, was the perfect opportunity. While some large U.S. companies couldn't focus on exporting because of the nature of their products (e.g., cement, fresh bread, electricity generation), we were well positioned for exports. Packaged cookies had a shelf life of four to six months, and crackers a full six months. Although potato chips had a shorter shelf life (three months), shipping them on a boat to Europe, even with some land-based shipping delays, would take just two weeks. I strongly believed there was no reason why every Snack Foods product couldn't be exported. Best of all, the markets in Europe were huge and seemingly under-served.

Another factor in favor of exporting was the unit cost reductions and margin-enhancing benefits that would come from capturing economies of scale through existing U.S. operations. Bottom line: exporting would lower production costs *and* increase sales. This was going to be great!

The moment I returned to my office, I placed a call to Ron's secretary Gladys. Bypassing Stu was a risk and a violation of *The Way*, but giving Stu the chance to kill this opportunity was an even bigger risk.

Gladys was protective of her boss's schedule, but she knew who I was and agreed to schedule me for fifteen minutes with Ron on the following Thursday. He and I knew each other on a first-name basis, but when I showed up for the meeting, Gladys still introduced me by my full name as she ushered me into the spacious corner office.

"How can I help you?" Ron looked up from the paperwork on his desk and focused on me.

My response was well rehearsed. "First, I wanted to thank you for the excellent presentation last week about our plans for 1988."

A slight grimace appeared on Ron's face. Was my brown-nosing so obvious?

After an awkward silence, I started talking again, hoping that saying something, anything, was better than a staring contest. "I especially loved what you said about exports. I've been thinking about this, and I firmly believe it's critical to our success."

"Is this why you wanted to see me? To thank me for my speech?"

I swallowed, then took the leap. "I'm here because I want to be part of the international initiative. I want to be on the team that puts the plans together. I've spent time in Europe, I speak French, and I want to take our cookies to Europe. In fact, a friend of mine just became president of his family's firm, the largest food distributor to grocery and convenience stores in France."

Ron sat back in his chair. "Interesting. I'm glad you came by. We need people like you if we're going to succeed internationally, but I also worry about distracting you from your current duties. You're a big asset here. Let me think about it. By the way, does Stu know you're here?"

I hedged my response. "He should."

Ron stood up, signaling the end of the meeting.

There was nothing to do then but wait. It was a gutsy thing I had done, and it would either make or break me.

Two weeks later, Gladys had me drop by to pick up an advance copy of an announcement. Paper-clipped to the memo was a handwritten note from Ron:

> *David,*
> *I think you'll be pleased with this announcement. Please listen carefully to and work closely with Stu Rogers, as he'll be heading this team. I know he'll appreciate having you on board. Meanwhile, keep up the good work on Chippers.*
> *Ron*

The memo, which was addressed to all Snack Foods managers, announced the formation of an international sales task force to be chaired by Stu Rogers. The task force included a representative from cookies (me), as well as from crackers, and potato chips. The fifth member of the task force was the Snack Foods VP of Finance. The task force's purpose was "to examine options for entering the markets of Europe, including exports *and* investments." The committee was to make recommendations in two months.

The Task Force Gets to Work

Stu never mentioned anything about my earlier meeting with Ron. Either Ron never told him or Stu decided to play it close to his vest. I suspected that Ron had maneuvered me onto the committee without telling Stu about my insubordination—another thing I will never forget about Ron.

Because I was the junior member of the team, I decided to play it cool. I didn't want to appear like a know-it-all, so I didn't promote Jacques's company as our French partner. I didn't even push for France as the first market we should enter.

The group met every Friday at 3 p.m., and the meetings were anything but harmonious. Stu seemed to enjoy the contention and squabbling for air-time. *Everyone* always had something to say. Meetings were supposed to end at 5 p.m., but they usually dragged on. I often wouldn't get home until 8 p.m. or later, mentally exhausted but satisfied with my contributions.

My one complaint about the process was that the task force didn't have access to good data. Going in, we understood that European farmers were highly subsidized by their governments, and that high tariff barriers would restrict the access of many imported processed food products. We also appreciated the confusing nature of government regulations. For example, a maze of different tariffs could be applied to bakery products, depending on sugar content and flour type, and rates varied from country to country.

Variations in food safety standards and labeling requirements quickly emerged as major concerns. Market differences were also pronounced throughout Europe and were driven by tastes that differed by country and region. We learned of the vast differences within Europe in the demand for fish, oils, nuts, bread products, cereals, and processed meats, but we had no idea how these differences would affect sales of our products. We had no idea how the checkerboard of rules was organized or how we could best play the game.

Beyond trade barriers and market differences, distribution differences were also common throughout Europe. Southern Europe, for example, was filled with many small family-owned grocery stores, which had limited shelf space, offered limited numbers of refrigerated products, and were notorious for poor inventory management. In contrast, the grocery retail chains in Northern Europe were more sophisticated and product marketing practices were more advanced. Given all of this, we debated how and where Snack Foods should organize itself to efficiently distribute products.

The task force discussed the data and the questions that our research raised. Some wondered if we should hire a consulting firm to collect more data and provide additional analyses and recommendations. Others argued that, while gathering more data might be valuable, the role of the task force was *not* to solve the exports riddle, but to make recommendations about the processes that product lines should follow. In other words, leave it to the product lines to figure out what research was important.

In my opinion, passing on the tough decisions was unacceptable. I argued for the creation of a new international department inside Snack Foods. Only by creating an organization that was fully charged with exporting could knowledge collection and interpretation ever work. An international department would be a resource to the product lines and a repository of best practices and data. I also hoped that an international department would be tasked with actually *buying* Snack Foods products internally and then selling the products overseas. The product lines couldn't lose with this approach. Sales would increase, and their attention could stay focused on their domestic customers. I was pleased when other members of the task force came to embrace my views.

On a Friday in late March, Stu presented our recommendations to Ron. The recommendations included:

- creation of an international department set up as a profit center headed by a vice president reporting to Ron Walker;

- granting the international department complete control over all international sales;
- tasking the department with buying products it deemed appropriate, at cost, from other divisions of Snack Foods; and
- granting the department authority to determine selling prices, distribution channels, etc. in overseas markets it considered attractive.

The recommendations were accepted, but only after a review by AFG's CEO. He received them favorably but decided to bring the matter to the board of directors for its stamp of approval. The board, too, went along with our recommendations.

A Department is Born

On June 3, 1988, the International Department was created. Stu Rogers was moved from his job running cookies and appointed general manager of the new department. He retained his title as vice president at Snack Foods. As for me, I was made head of strategic planning at the International Department, reporting to Stu, and given a 40 percent pay raise.

We determined that the first exports would include four products: Chocolate Chippers, Scotland's Own cookies, Wheats-a-Lot crackers, and Crunchers BBQ potato chips. These were Snack Foods' four best-selling brands. We decided that initial sales would be made to U.S. government agencies that could stock the brands (free of import controls) on military bases and in embassy commissaries. By the end of 1987, international sales had reached $398,000.

At this point, I decided to push the opportunity with Jacques's firm and with France, in particular. Behind the scenes, Jacques had already been helpful in sorting out the regulations, tariffs, and other trade barriers we faced as exporters.

Based on GDP and GDP per capita levels, my research and development efforts focused on four other countries: the U.K., Germany, Switzerland, and Italy. Discussions with trade representatives at U.S. embassies in these countries, as well as meetings with the branch offices of the American Chambers of Commerce, led me to lists of possible distributors. After a six-city interview tour that we conducted in the spring of 1988, contracts were signed with distributors in London, Munich, and Milan, in addition to the partnership with Jacques's company that would cover France and Switzerland. Each was well regarded as a distributor of processed food products, and all of them had solid, long-term relationships with major grocery retailers.

Each distributor was provided with our pricing for the four products at the center of Snack Foods' export drive. For each product, a chart was organized that indicated decreasing per-unit prices as sales volumes increased. Distributors were free to buy what they wanted and sell at whatever price they deemed appropriate. Because of the price breaks, they were incentivized to maximize sales. Each was given exclusive rights to its country's markets for a period of three years.

A Slow Start

To my surprise, sales to all four distributors amounted to less than $3 million by the end of 1989. It was a big disappointment. A review of the sales data indicated that over 90 percent of our products were going to a small number of American grocery stores in cities with substantial U.S. expat populations. Every major European city seemed to have one or two stores catering to Americans hungry for peanut butter, Jell-O and root beer. The prices were notoriously high, often three or four times as much as locally sourced products. The model our distributors seemed to be following was to pay high duties on the imports and then slap a new label on the product.

Importing products in this manner was usually enough to clear the regulatory hurdles, but was notoriously inefficient and largely ineffective. Not only were sales minimal, but we also discovered that no efforts were being made to look for cracks in the trade regulations. Also, low sales volumes were discouraging our distributors and the retailers from making any significant investment in our products. Their lack of commitment to (or knowledge of) our products was embarrassing. Given the limited number and small size of American grocery stores in Europe, something had to be done to turn things around.

Jacques's business was the one exception. He knew that chocolate chip cookies and other sweets weren't likely to do well in France, but as we'd discussed in New York two years earlier, he also knew that crackers would be a great complement to cheese consumed in his country. He correctly believed that the old-fashioned image conveyed by our packaging would be a good selling point.

Jacques used his connections to help AFG penetrate Belgium and the Netherlands with our hard, salty pretzels. Consumers in these countries drank lots of beer, and the small pretzels were a nice accompaniment. The most helpful wholesalers in these countries were the mom-and-pop outfits that distributed to restaurants and pubs, but unfortunately, they did not distribute to the major grocery stores. While these countries were outside Jacques's official territory, I did not raise this as an issue because sales were being directed through his Paris warehouse. I did put Jacques on notice that his export sales to these countries would be subject to review if and when Snack Foods formally opened up additional countries in Europe.

CHAPTER

10

THE WAY

"HEY, SORRY THE CALL TOOK LONGER THAN I THOUGHT IT WOULD," JACQUES said as he joined me out on the deck. "Beautiful views, no?"

"Spectacular."

"Are you ready to continue our discussion?"

"*Absolument.*"

Whatever was happening in Jacques's company must have been brought under control because the three of them picked up where we left off without missing a beat.

Anjanette stepped up to the screen. "So at some point companies discover that the customers in foreign markets who will accept standardized exports—let's call them *export accepters*—are typically fewer than those who want the products customized or tailored to their needs. We'll call them *export rejecters*. To penetrate into this larger segment of customers, companies typically have to make investments and set up operations abroad. This moves them into Stage 3: internationalization." Anjanette again projected on the flat screen the diagram that Hans had shown earlier (see Figure 10-1).

Figure 10-1

Stages on the Path of Globalization

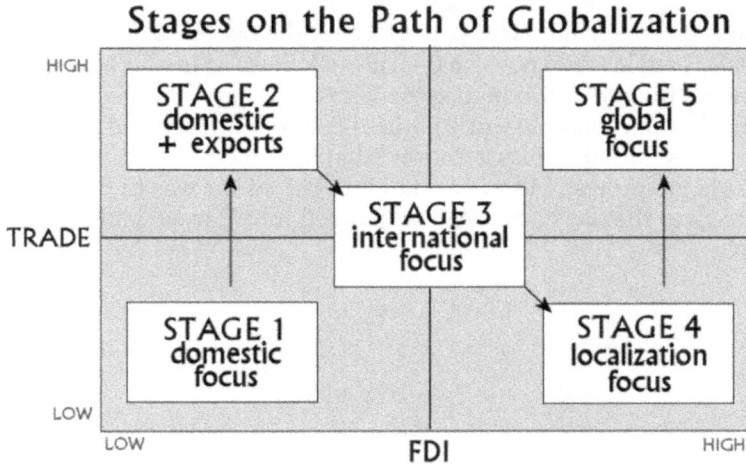

"Yes," I said, "I was heavily involved in our first efforts in this."

"This is what Jacques told me. You may not like what I am about to tell you about mistakes that many companies make at this stage."

I grimaced but indicated she should go on.

"Part of the reason companies can move into this next stage is they have been successful at exports. But, what makes them successful at exports?"

I almost answered before I realized it was a rhetorical question.

"Three things make companies good at exports. First, they standardize their products to capture cost savings. Second, they standardize their production processes to ensure consistent quality and to capture cost savings. Third, they ingrain their culture into their employees in order to get consistent behavior from them. In other words, they standardize their product, process, and people. They create—"

"The Way," I said, before she could finish her sentence. "The AFG Way, or more specifically the Snack Foods Way, has been a huge part of our success."

"Yes. But I am going to suggest, based on our research of other companies, that it is also part of the reason for Snack Foods' current struggles."

I frowned and leaned forward.

Anjanette held up a calming hand. "Before you get upset, let me explain. Because The Way is seen as the path to success, the firm sends expatriate managers who know and embrace The Way and expects them to follow it wherever they decide to set up operations. They do this precisely to ensure that the new local employees learn and obey The Way and that they do this without equivocation.

"Unfortunately, there are two problems with this. First, companies typically go into the new market and hire people who are pliable and seem most likely to conform to The Way. Second, the people they *need* to hire are actually people who know what local customers want and how to make the key adjustments in products to penetrate the *export rejecter* segment of the market. The complacent go-with-the-flow adherents of The Way— who tend to get hired—are not exactly what is needed."

I wanted to protest, but in my gut I recognized she was right. My mind drifted back to the days when AFG expanded into Europe and my role in that move.

CHAPTER

11

AFG'S ROAD TO EUROPE

BY 1990, IT WAS CLEAR THAT SNACK FOODS WOULD NEVER PENETRATE DEEP-ly into international markets solely by exporting and working with distrib-utors. To succeed, we needed to get closer to our customers to understand their taste preferences. With better insights, we could make adjustments ranging from new product formulations to packaging.

Back then, it was clear to me Snack Foods would have to set up physi-cal operations overseas. Few of my colleagues thought this was either de-sirable or necessary. Only a handful of managers inside the International Department appreciated the large, untapped pool of potential customers lying underneath our easy export acceptors, who bought our products mostly out of curiosity. Outside the International Department, the vast majority of AFG executives didn't give a fig about export customers. They were entirely focused on the U.S., the world's largest market for food, where they locked horns every day with our competitors.

The shortsightedness of these executives drove me mad. To me, it was crystal clear that Europeans, especially those in our selected markets, had lots of money to spend and that European sales could have a big impact on Snack Foods' overall revenues. Capturing this potential meant adjusting to more localized preferences. Trying to access European customers via ex-ports working their way through a labyrinth of trade barriers would never produce meaningful sales.

Stu Rogers and I both came to this conclusion less than six months after the formation of the International Department. However, it took other senior leaders at Snack Foods more than a year to recognize the merits of investing real money in overseas operations. After months of meeting and lobbying, some of the senior executives at HQ reluctantly agreed that if Snack Foods were to grow in Europe, it would have to surrender some economies of scale at home, establish operations overseas, and make adjustment to the products.

The Expansion Begins

Snack Foods' direct foreign investment happened over an extended period, but it started in earnest in 1991. At first, our existing distributors were furious. They feared they would lose the rights to sell the Snack Foods product line. When we reminded them that their existing rights to particular country markets excluded other distributors but *not* Snack Foods itself, they backed down. Also, I pointed out, they could continue as our distributors, and nobody would take this away from them—as long as they were doing a good job. Moreover, by manufacturing our products in Europe, we would leapfrog tariff barriers, lowering *their* costs and improving *their* profit margins. They liked that.

After much debate over where to build our first plant, the higher sales we were achieving in France made the decision pretty obvious for us. We would build the plant just outside Lyon in south-central France.

Both Ron Walker and AFG's CEO were nervous about the investment. Although they accepted the need to make some adjustments in product formulation and packaging, they continued to worry about the risks of going global. It wasn't just about money. Ron was concerned about eroding the standards espoused by *The Way*, and he insisted that tried and true processes should be preserved in any and all international operations. To both Ron and AFG's CEO, *The Way* had made Snack Foods the success that it was.

When determining who should lead the first international operation, the senior team insisted on an exemplar of *The Way*, a leader who would spread the gospel to the benighted locals. Hal Butler was selected as the first general manager for Snack Foods Europe. Hal was 52 and had spent the first four years of his career at General Mills in Minneapolis before coming to AFG 25 years ago. Since then, he'd worked in operations, first inventory management and then manufacturing. He'd even headed a couple of factories in the U.S. No one personified *The Way* better than Hal.

I landed the job as VP of sales and marketing for the new venture.

Seven other individuals would be sent to Lyon as part of our executive team. We would all be on three to five year assignments. If the venture went as planned, the team members expected Snack Foods would make additional investments in an expanding number of countries. The pioneers would be rewarded with overseeing additional AFG activities across

Europe.

In addition to the management team, AFG would send another approximately thirty people for shorter periods. They would contribute specific technical capabilities and knowledge.

The Home Front

On the home front, Sarah greeted news of my promotion and transfer with as much enthusiasm as a seal greets a polar bear. Sarah had quit her job when our first daughter was born, and with the birth of our second in the last year, she was happily on her way to becoming a career soccer mom. She didn't speak French, had never visited France, and had misgivings about being thousands of miles from her family. "My mom will never get to see the girls."

"Your mom can come visit any time she wants." I went on to praise the climate and culture of Lyon and emphasized that this was a big opportunity. What I did *not* emphasize was the potential for a longer-term regional role in Europe, since I didn't want her to think we'd be living in France forever. She could entertain the idea of spending three years there, but a longer stay was more than what she would likely accept—for now.

In March 1991, Sarah and I parked the girls with her mother and flew to Paris and then Lyon for a look-see visit. I wanted to find housing for the family and give Sarah a feel for France. We arrived on a beautiful spring day. Lyon was much more tranquil than Sarah had expected. Near the city center was a beautiful park, *Parc de la Tête d'Or*. The *Saône*, a picturesque river, ran through the city and, though it wasn't as mighty as the Mississippi, had its charm. In fact, we liked the city center so much that we decided to take our time getting to know the area so we could find a home near all the right amenities. In the end, we rented a three-bedroom apartment at *La Reine Astrid* on *boulevard des Belges*, a few minutes' walk from both the river and the park. Sarah seemed happy and even excited when we signed the lease.

By the time the movers packed up our apartment in St. Louis, Sarah's mood had shifted. She was sad about moving so far from friends and family and again apprehensive about living in France. When I tried to cheer her up, she agreed that Lyon had its charms and that the move would be an interesting adventure. Meanwhile, our oldest daughter (four years old at the time) was bouncing off the walls with excitement about flying all night on an airplane. Our youngest was too young to notice or care.

It took six weeks for our furniture to arrive from home. During our first two weeks in Lyon, we lived in a hotel. There is nothing like sharing a cramped hotel room or trying to enjoy a traditional two-hour dinner at a French restaurant with two pre-school children to make you beg for an end to the adventure.

The next four weeks we spent in our new apartment, waiting for furniture that seemed like it would never arrive in port or clear customs. We purchased some basic supplies and hunkered down—at least we had a kitchen and some space. Once the furniture was delivered to the apartment, we were able to relax a bit more. Or at least Sarah was able to relax. I still had a mountain of work to do.

I kept telling Sarah that the best part of the move was my generous financial package. Although living costs in Lyon were about 30 percent more than in St. Louis, my compensation was nearly double. Sarah was sure we could save enough for a down payment on a house when we returned to the U.S.

CHAPTER

12

EXPATS ON PARADE

IN MAY 1991, SHORTLY AFTER MY ARRIVAL IN LYON, THE TEAM ASSEMBLED and set out to establish the new international operation in France. Because we wanted to get this first expansion right, Snack Foods sent and maintained twice the number of expatriate managers as our international assignment consultant had said was the norm at other benchmark companies. This cost more, but both Ron Walker and Hal Butler wanted to ensure that the operation didn't go native. It was vital that we stick to *The Way*. As a consequence, the locals we hired were chosen for their willingness to learn and conform to the Snack Foods culture and approach to business.

To screen job candidates for manufacturing and sales positions (about 70 percent of the workforce), we initially conducted interviews using interpreters. Within a short time, however, we concluded that all of our employees should be able to speak conversational English. To fill the management slots, we hired local recruitment firms, asking them to weed out candidates who didn't speak English well enough, or who were too opinionated, too proud, or too headstrong, i.e., "too French." Of course, we didn't use that phrase. Despite this admonition to the headhunters, we were still forced to pay close attention to hiring, as most of the candidates proved far from suitable.

One interviewee in particular came to personify every quality we *did not* want to see in our local managers. To fill the new position of VP of Quality Control, Hal interviewed four candidates, all French. He asked me and five other members of the expat team to individually interview them after he was finished. We had a set interview script to follow. After this was over, we all submitted our comments and impressions. I wrote the following about a candidate named Pierre Ovrard:

> *My first impression of Pierre was very positive. He had attended one of the elite French universities and had excellent experience within Groupe Danone, the French dairy and nutrition giant. At first, he seemed to give all the right answers to the questions I posed: why he wanted the job, what he could contribute, etc. But as the interview progressed, I could see that he wasn't forthcoming about why he wanted to leave Danone. People in his position tend to leave for a reason, but he avoided any discussion of this. He wouldn't even make eye contact.*

When I asked about his expectation of a typical workweek, he said that 35 hours of work per week was enough. "If you can't get it done in 35 hours, it isn't worth doing." He then joked, "You Americans work so hard because you are less efficient than us French." I didn't find this funny.

Toward the end of the interview, he seemed to think the job was his and began offering unsolicited advice on our recruitment efforts. Among other things, he stressed the importance of hiring engineers who had attended only the top French schools, the need to offer higher pay and benefits to induce managers to work for a foreign firm, and that we hire union workers and track their hours in accordance with French law. When I asked if he had any more suggestions, he shrugged and said, "I will assume that, as a manager, I will get the usual six weeks of holiday at full pay. *N'est pas vrai?*"

When I reported my findings to Hal, he replied, "You're the only person who uncovered this. Everyone else on the team stuck to the basic interview protocol which didn't include some of the questions you asked. Hiring this guy would be a big mistake. You may have really saved our bacon." My report got other members of the management team to broaden their questions. Finding candidates who fit Snack Foods' culture proved tougher than we had anticipated at the outset.

Meeting the Challenges

Launching the French office and the manufacturing operation evolved into a nightmare, mostly because we didn't know what we were doing. Despite our best recruitment efforts, we were left with mediocre employees, and once operations started, many managers and employees devoted more energy to making excuses for their poor performances than to efforts at improvement. In the early days, we had to fire a few, while most of them did just enough work to avoid being fired. The pervasive attitude of the French seemed to be that Americans demanded too much of their employees.

The one thing that kept us sane during this period was the knowledge that we had a great product line and powerful Snack Foods systems. These core strengths freed us to adjust to and learn about the local rules and procedures.

In November, five months after the team arrived in Europe, Hal received the green light to replicate the French start-up in Germany, Italy, and the U.K. Rather than overwhelm the team with simultaneous start-ups, Hal decided to phase them in. In June 1992, the German office opened in Munich, followed by full manufacturing in September of that year. In January 1993, Snack Foods opened its U.K. office in Birmingham, followed two months later by full manufacturing. And in the fall of 1993, Italy came online, also with sales and manufacturing facilities.

Expatriate U.S. general managers staffed each country office. Rather than re-invent the wheel in each locale, Hal organized a regional HQ start-up advisory team based in Lyon. Members of the team included five Lyon-based U.S. expats who had been heavily involved in the start-up in France. Later, the team was expanded to include two other Americans who were involved in the German start-up.

CHAPTER
13

BE CAREFUL WHAT YOU WISH FOR

JACQUES'S VOICE SNAPPED ME BACK INTO THE MOMENT. "I SEE BY THE EX-pression on your face you recall you also hired, I think you call them, 'yes men,' when you set up early operations in France and elsewhere."

"I wouldn't exactly call them 'yes men.'"

"No? Okay. Perhaps that is too harsh, but they were not the type to challenge you or to give you really deep or critical insights into the market."

"You're right, but I think I am hearing you say that hiring them was a mistake and was my fault."

"No. I am not saying it was your fault. I am saying that it is a very common mistake made for understandable but misguided reasons. It is understandable and common that any firm would send people it knows and trusts to watch over its new investments in foreign lands. However, the problem is that when these expatriates hire primarily those who will conform to *The Way*, whether it is the *AFG Way* or the *Toyota Way*, the company loses (or discards) the insights into the local market that they actually need to move successfully into the internationalization stage."

Anjanette took her cue and began again. "Often the expats sent to set up the new operations do not realize that the people they purposely hired are exactly *not* the people they need to help them penetrate the new market. Some firms never confront this reality and fail to make big gains in international sales beyond exports. They never move past Stage 2. To some extent this is true of many of the Japanese firms. Part of the reason they have fallen so far down the *Global Fortune 500* list is that, in relative terms, they simply have failed to capture the foreign sales that their competitors from Europe and North America have experienced in the markets they entered."

While this was somewhat painful to hear, I tried to make the issue impersonal. "So you have to be careful what you wish for. If you wish for and hire people to fit in, that is exactly what you will get, when what you need is people who will help you get what you don't have—insights into the local market and the changes and adaptations you need to make to penetrate the market."

"David, *mon ami*, this is why I made you the offer to come work for me. When you see things from a new angle, you are willing to move on in a new way."

At this point, I felt less chastised. I recalled with a more critical eye what happened after our early efforts to open operations in Europe.

CHAPTER

14

NEW JOB, OLD PERSPECTIVE

IN THE SPRING OF 1994, HAL RETIRED AFTER A LARGELY SUCCESSFUL TEN-
ure. At 61, he was looking forward to less stress and more time with his
grandchildren.

Shortly thereafter, I was asked to meet with Division President Ron
Walker in St. Louis, where I learned that Hal had strongly endorsed me as
his replacement.

"Like Hal, I'm pleased with the progress that Snack Foods is making in
Europe," said Ron. "If you accept the job, I want you to stay in Lyon, at
least for now."

I nodded, wondering if I could sell an additional stint in Lyon to Sarah.

Ron leaned back in his chair. "I expect you to grow the business in
Europe by 50 percent a year over the next five years. That may sound like
a lot, but keep in mind you're starting from a small base."

"It'll take a lot of hard work, but I think we can manage at least 50
percent."

Ron nodded. "Listen, you won't reach that target by selling more cookies in just four countries. You need to branch out. Why aren't we in Spain
or Greece or The Netherlands or Sweden?"

"We're feeling our way. Each market has its own challenges."

Ron rose and held out his hand. "I want an answer by the end of the day on whether you'll take this job."

I shook his hand. "Thank you, Ron. I appreciate your confidence in me."

"When you say 'yes,' as I know you will"—he smiled and winked—"we'll meet again. Tomorrow. I want to hear your plans to take this organization forward."

I left Ron's office, floating on air, and called Sarah in France to report the news.

"You'd be crazy not to take the job," her voice reflected my own excitement. "But," she paused, "I need to tell you right now that Lyon's charm is wearing thin. Can you move the regional headquarters to England? I could handle that for a few more years."

"Well, maybe. Honey, they may speak English in England, but I guarantee that the food and weather are much better in Lyon. I can't necessarily promise a move to England—"

"It sounds like the chances of moving to England are about the same as taking that second honeymoon to Bora Bora. To be honest, I'm ready to go home. And, the sooner the better." She sounded like a spoilt child, but she'd been such a good sport for the past three years.

I swallowed the sharp arguments on the tip of my tongue. "I couldn't have done any of this without you. You know that."

"Don't try to sweet-talk me. That's how you got me over here in the first place."

We both laughed.

Sarah asked, "What about salary? How much more will you be making?"

"I have no idea." I laughed at that, too. "It never occurred to me to ask."

Sarah didn't laugh this time. "If you're going to take on the regional responsibility, they owe you."

"Of course. I'm sure Ron will be fair."

"Hold out for generous." Her tone took on a more serious note. "The sacrifices I'm willing to make are not limitless."

After lunch, I walked back to Ron's office. His assistant said that he was in a meeting and couldn't be interrupted.

"Let him know that David came by." I cleared my throat. "Tell him the answer is yes."

She gave me a confused look.

I grinned. "He'll understand."

I walked away the General Manager of Snack Foods for Europe. I was 34 years old. It was 1994.

CHAPTER

15

BIG PLANS, HARSH REALITIES

HAVING COMMITTED TO THE PROMOTION AND STAYING IN EUROPE, I WORKED through the night preparing for my meeting with Ron. The next morning I met again with Ron and outlined a four-point plan for Snack Foods Europe, focusing on:

- more products
- more communicative packaging
- more distribution channels, yielding
- more sales and profits

It was my intention, I explained, to expand the number of products offered, the range of channels in which they were sold (including big box retailers), and the number of countries in which they were distributed. I also wanted to overcome local resistance to products deemed too American. I planned to achieve the latter by Europeanizing not just formulations of some of the products, but also their packaging and advertising approaches. When I returned to France, my first step would be to tour the operations in every country where we had manufacturing plants and to hold extensive discussions with the country heads about what was working, what wasn't, and how we could turn things around. I was upbeat about my odds for success, and my super-charged optimism must have been infectious.

Plan Approved

Ron asked a few pointed questions, but none seemed to indicate a great understanding of the realities of our business in Europe. His queries were mostly good business questions, the kind that a consultant would ask when scoping out a project. At the end of our hour together, he approved my plan and offered his full support.

Implementing my plan proved easier said than done. One of the most intractable problems we faced was the sheer variety of taste preferences from country to country across Europe, as well as general unfamiliarity with certain snack foods that were common in the U.S. For example, we promoted a range of cookies, from chocolate chip and peanut butter to oatmeal-raisin. The French hated peanut butter, so 70 percent of peanut butter cookies in France sat on the shelves past their expiration dates, leading store owners to demand that we pull them. In Germany and the U.K., all of our cookies were fairly popular, but retailers griped that Snack Foods wasn't doing enough to promote them.

Our brownies—plain, with nuts, and with frosting—were not selling well in any market. We thought that offering three different varieties would solve the national taste preferences problem. Instead, these choices confused people. Europeans were not accustomed to eating brownies. The French didn't like frosting on their snack foods. And the labeling was inadequate. Some consumers complained that there were too many nuts in the "brownies with nuts." They considered these nut cakes, not brownies.

Despite these problems, I enjoyed some successes during my first two years as General Manager, Europe. Sales of all cookies increased by an average of 43 percent and sales of crackers by 51 percent on an annual basis. Not bad, but we all recognized that we were still operating from a small base. We achieved the uptick by supporting the bestselling brands with more advertising expenditures in the markets where they were doing well, along with repackaging the promising but poorly performing products in key markets. For example, there was no reason that our Frisco brand crackers couldn't achieve greater success in cheese-and-cracker-loving France other than that they were hampered by stereotyping as a fat-filled American junk food. To compensate, we developed new labeling and packaging that began dismantling Frisco's image as too buttery and too foreign. While the numbers were a bit below Ron's expectations, we were happy with our progress. He seemed pleased as well.

CHAPTER

16

HITTING THE BRICK WALL

IN 1996, WE HIT A BRICK WALL. SALES GROWTH STALLED. INSTEAD OF 40 AND 50 percent growth, we slipped to single-digit increases for both cookies and crackers. I placed the blame squarely on the shoulders of our local European managers, few of whom seemed to show any initiative or leadership. Most were doers and not leaders. Yes, they did what they were told, but many also complained that it was very hard to achieve their desired targets. This was by far their most irritating trait, since we had hoped these managers would offer insights into the minds of local consumers. Instead, they didn't have a clue why our sales weren't growing. When asked for ideas and opinions, they shrugged their shoulders and mostly remained silent.

It was obvious that I needed a more talented and assertive crew. It now seemed clear that we would never regain our momentum and move forward with the current crop of leaders. It was time for a management shake-up.

At the time, the reason we had "yes men" was entirely lost on me. I did not understand that the lousy leaders we had were exactly the people *we* had recruited when we started. We had deliberately avoided hiring managers who were too local, too opinionated, and who would not easily conform to *The Way*. As I looked back now, I could see that they hadn't changed, but our needs had.

Lacking this insight, and too busy to personally oversee a search for new candidates, I retained local search firms to help find and hire high-caliber local leaders. I needed people who understood the markets. I was shocked when most of the qualified candidates demanded compensation packages at least 50 percent higher than their Snack Foods counterparts in the U.S. and 75 to 100 percent higher than the European managers already working for us. While I was none too pleased with having to pay exorbitant salaries to induce talented locals to join us, I had no choice. I reluctantly agreed to the terms.

This was not the end of my challenges. After the new leaders were hired, I became concerned that these managers, while technically proficient, were prone to adopting practices and approaches that were too European in terms of employee policies, supervision, and new product introductions. I had learned that the problems we were encountering weren't limited to just the new hires but seemed endemic *to all* European managers.

By this point, I had come to dislike most European ways of doing business. Among other things, Snack Foods wasn't allowed to fire people at will, since almost every country had socialist labor policies that made it impossible to get rid of malcontents or incompetents. Because of this, we simply passed over the old contingent of local managers and brought in people above them. The remaining dead wood boosted our costs and negatively played on employee morale.

"And they wonder why Europeans aren't as productive as Americans," I complained one day to Sarah at home. "They've got higher taxes, red tape wrapped around everything, and ossified traditions and prejudices that even *they* can't explain—except to say, 'This is how things are done in France, Italy, or Spain.' I can't *tell* you how tired I am of hearing that excuse!"

Sarah was kind enough to not say, "I told you so."

The most frustrating aspect of the situation was there wasn't much I could do about it. As it stood, I was so busy micromanaging the first wave of local managers that I had no time to adopt and manage a second group. And now I realized the leadership problem wasn't limited to individuals but encompassed the whole business culture. What *could* I do? At that point, I was focused on how I could get Frenchmen, Germans, Italians, Spaniards, and others to embrace the *Snack Foods Way* and become true company leaders.

CHAPTER

17

ONWARD AND UPWARD

NOTWITHSTANDING OUR ONGOING LEADERSHIP CHALLENGES, BY EARLY 1997 operations had begun an upturn. Sales growth returned and was projected to increase by 25 percent during the year. Snack Foods now had offices and manufacturing in eight European countries. In Germany, we had three manufacturing facilities (Munich, Berlin and Dusseldorf); in France, four manufacturing facilities (Paris, Lyon, Rennes and Marseille); in Italy, two facilities (Milan and Rome); and in the U.K., we had three (London, Birmingham and Glasgow). Austria, Switzerland, Greece and Turkey had one manufacturing plant apiece. The factories were mostly running smoothly, and, slowly but surely, our products were finding a home in more and more retail outlets.

That year I was on the road a lot. I ran from business-class flights to waiting limousines to the nearest Hilton, and from there to every local headquarters. I toured factories, met distributors, and visited with customers. At year's end, my assistant informed me that I'd been out of town for a total of 174 days.

Sarah's patience was wearing thin. My schedule and my failure to arrange a move to the U.K. chipped away at her good will. She grew ever more eager to leave France. Whenever I was home, she complained about nearly everything under the French sun. The kitchen was too small, especially the nine-cubic-foot refrigerator. She hated that French homes didn't come with closets and that she had to buy closets from furniture stores and assemble them by herself because I wasn't around. She'd never gotten over the fact that the king-size bed we brought from the U.S. didn't fit in the bedroom and had to be thrown out. We didn't have a garage and had to park the car outside, which meant it was covered in frost in the winter. She didn't like the car because, like most French cars, it had a stick shift. The international school was a 30-minute drive from the house, and there was no bus service for the kids, which meant she had to spend two hours per day ferrying kids back and forth—driving a car she hated through big city traffic. She was lonely and bored. She was friends with just a couple of other American expatriates, and when she was alone, there was no American TV she could watch. While her French had improved, it was far from fluent. Understanding French TV or reading a newspaper was nearly impossible and was a constant source of frustration. Telephone calls to the U.S. were expensive, and there was no Internet in those days.

I didn't blame Sarah for feeling the way she did. After nearly seven years in Europe, I began signaling to Ron that I was ready to return to the U.S.

Sarah wanted the kids to attend school back home. Their French was nearly perfect, and they were starting to think of themselves as French. They were losing some of their American identity—or at least that was the feedback to Sarah from her parents. In addition, her parents were getting on in years, and she worried about living nine time zones away. She complained that the girls were growing up without a father and that maybe a move to the U.S. would allow me to see more of them. She had a point. Although my time in France had been challenging and professionally rewarding, I empathized with Sarah and the girls and their difficulties.

"I can't take much more of this," Sarah blurted out one night. "Living over here was an adventure at first, but these last few years, it's more like being in exile."

"I know, I know." I put a hand on her shoulder. "Give it a few more months. Gossip is flying that AFG's current CEO will be retiring soon, and Ron is sure to take his place." I slipped my arm around her and gave her a hug. "You know the guy loves me. Rumors are flying that I'll be named head of Snack Foods, and then we can move back to the States."

She pulled away from my offered comfort. "I hope you're right." She frowned. "I *really* hope you're right."

CHAPTER
18

AN ERA OF NEW LEADERSHIP

I *WAS* RIGHT.

In January 1998, Ron was named the CEO of AFG. His promotion reflected the board's recognition of the great performance of Snack Foods. During Ron's tenure, the division had increased revenues nearly twice as fast as the next-best performing division, Agribusiness, and its profits were now five times greater than AFG's largest division, Bakery.

Ron had a free hand in choosing his successor and, though his choice required approval from the AFG board of directors, he had little trouble persuading them that I was the perfect candidate. He argued that I'd performed admirably in Europe, supervising the opening of dozens of sales offices and seventeen factories across the continent. He assured them that I had spread *The Way* throughout the organization and Snack Foods' systems were well entrenched and running smoothly. The board approved his recommendation.

In February 1998, I assumed my new role.

As head of AFG's global snack foods business, my responsibilities included Europe and North America (Canada/U.S.), plus new operations that had opened in Latin America (Brazil, Argentina, Mexico, Chile), and Asia Pacific (Japan, Hong Kong, Singapore, Thailand, Australia, and the

Philippines). The job represented a huge new challenge, one that came with a personal staff of seven people and a 500-square-foot office on the executive floor at corporate HQ in St. Louis. My salary nearly tripled, and my variable pay had the potential to add even more to my take-home. At the age of 38, I was the youngest division head in the company's history. On the downside, the new position would require frequent trips within the US as well as abroad. The trips to Europe would typically require more time and more distance than those I'd taken in the past. No longer could I take a day and visit our offices in Germany. Instead, I would need to combine it with other country visits. This would sometimes require me to be gone from home for two weeks or longer.

Staffing Issues

There was also the question of who would replace me as GM of Europe. During my time as the regional head, I'd learned that in order to penetrate European markets we had to make bigger changes in product formulation and packaging than we'd anticipated. We arrived in Europe thinking our products would sell themselves. We didn't place enough emphasis on educating our distribution channels and consumers. It was a hard lesson. Our biggest mistake was introducing our product lines to the entire European market. We had better success when we adapted to local taste preferences.

For example, we extended the Frisco cracker line to include varieties that replaced butter with Italian olive oil. Then we learned that the Spanish prefer Spanish olive oil and the Greeks prefer Greek olive oil. While the British loved all of our cookies, including the peanut butter kind, the Germans preferred less refined varieties containing nuts and raisins, while the French preferred highly refined cookies. Heaven forbid that anyone in France would like the same thing that the Germans or the British or the Italians enjoyed.

We had *hoped* our local managers would bring with them a deeper understanding of these issues and advise us on necessary adaptations. If this had been the case, it would be easy to argue that the GM of Europe should be a European. But it wasn't the case. Instead, too many of the locals offered us the worst of both worlds: not enough input on how we could tailor our products and our advertising to local markets and too much Euro-centric attitude. All too often our managers seemed to think that anything and everything invented in the U.S. was lousy and should be rejected.

A New GM for Europe

After a thorough review of candidates, in late 1998 I hired long-time AFG executive Bill Kramer as my replacement. I had known Bill for many years. He was American, smart, and highly disciplined in his approach to decision making. He was a fact-based decision maker, a trait that I knew would be critically important. He was just the kind of guy we needed to bring more structure and order to Snack Foods in Europe. This would be Bill's first international assignment and likely his last job in the company. At 58, he was close to retirement. Bill had spent his adult life in St. Louis, first with Monsanto and then, for the past 26 years with AFG. He was one of the few executives who was legitimately good enough to move from Bakery to Snack Foods. His most recent position in Snack Foods was as Chief Controller, a job that included regulating and monitoring financial flows and some production volumes. He took over my office in Lyon while his wife remained in St. Louis.

When I asked about this arrangement, Bill raised his eyebrows and said, "It isn't ideal, but after 34 years of marriage, we don't mind being apart every now and then." He went on to explain that his wife had her own career, and that their grandchildren were in St. Louis.

That made some sense.

Bill continued, "I'll be home once a month for our executive team meetings. She'll come over on her vacations or for a short trip every now and then. We decided it would be easier to manage our lives this way, at least for a few years."

After his arrival in Lyon, Bill spent most of his time coordinating with headquarters in St. Louis and reporting on the performance improvements. He didn't introduce any major changes to the systems I'd installed.

He explained, "David, your job was to put everything in place. Mine is to tighten the screws, improve the quality of data collected, and make sure our standards for financial performance and production efficiencies are met."

I couldn't have agreed more. This is exactly why I chose him.

CHAPTER

19

TIGHTENING THE SCREWS

ONE OF BILL'S FIRST TASKS WAS TO FILL THE ONGOING AND NEW HOLES IN management. When I returned to St. Louis, I brought back with me my former director of Marketing for Europe, Stan Bench. Bill would need a new top marketing guy. He decided the European head of technical support was not up to U.S. standards, so he transferred the man back to his native Germany and searched for a replacement. When he tried to work with the regional HR manager to fill these slots, Bill found she could not provide recruiting assistance outside her native France. In fact, he discovered that her regional position was only part-time; she actually held a full-time position in the French subsidiary. So Bill decided to add a new HR manager to his list of senior hires.

Bill turned to Spencer Stuart, Inc., a global head-hunting firm, to help fill these and other slots. He used their office in London to lead the search, in part because of the language affinity, but also because he appreciated Spencer Stuart's global reach and talent pool.

Within three months, he had a new European director of marketing and sales (Miguel Alvarez, from Spain), a new manager of human resources (Anne Lingley from London), and a new director of finance (Robert Boedeker from Holland).

Once the new hires settled in to their positions, Bill found additional organizational and staffing changes were needed—all normal in a maturing organization. A year into the job, he approved a replacement for the number two person in manufacturing and agreed to organize European sales into three sub-regions. Each would be directed by a new regional head of sales: one for the Nordics, the U.K. and Ireland; another for central Europe (France, Germany, and the Benelux); and a third to supervise southern Europe (Italy, Greece, Spain, Portugal and Turkey).

Dealing with Politics

Every major hiring decision required Bill's approval and general buy-in from me in St. Louis. Still, he didn't like all the subtleties and behind-the-scenes maneuvering that seemed to happen in Europe around major decisions. I guess I had grown used to it, so it didn't bother me as much. Bill was a "say what you mean, and mean what you say" kind of guy. The subtleties of the French and their love of rules, debate, and politics, as well as the vague and indirect communication style of the Spanish, drove him nuts. So he relied on his European direct reports to work things out and bring him final hiring recommendations.

Behind-the-scenes discussions and implicit agreements were nothing new for the German, Italian and U.K. managers. They had experienced this both in their previous jobs at name-brand European corporations and during their time at Snack Foods Europe. They believed that back-and-forth and back-channel discussions were the key to making needed changes and adjustments. This extended not only into hiring decisions but also decisions touching on operations and strategy.

Local Initiatives

It is difficult to say whether the change in European leadership was responsible or not, but during Bill's first year in Lyon, local and regional managers became more assertive in their views of product choices and marketing strategies in Europe.

On one occasion, they pushed and finally won approval from Bill for a product to be launched in Northern Europe that didn't even exist in the U.S. It was a combination wafer, hazelnut, and chocolate-covered cookie. The local team took considerable pride in this accomplishment and the fact that in its first year, the cookie became our top-selling brand in the Netherlands, Norway, and Sweden. That same year it was number two in Germany and Austria.

Not every local initiative produced positive results, and even when they did, the other country managers often ignored the lessons learned. For example, our U.K. affiliate had what we believed the best practices in customer relationship management. Even though Bill encouraged the other managers to study the U.K. model, none of the other country GMs followed up. Furthermore, the U.K. country GM wasn't particularly interested in sharing what he was doing, since his performance was assessed on *his* country's performance, not on other countries' performances and certainly *not* on how well he mentored his management brethren in other parts of Europe.

In one report, Bill told me our plant in Turkey enjoyed labor costs that were 72 percent lower than in Switzerland. When I asked if there were efforts under way to rationalize production, Bill agreed that this would be ideal but said that opposition from the Swiss was proving difficult to overcome. I also learned that our Austrian team wasn't aware of what the German team was doing with packaging and had allocated millions of dollars to duplicate what was essentially exactly what the Germans had done.

I must admit that though similar problems existed while I was in Europe, I had largely overlooked them or lacked the data that Bill had assembled. Rather, I focused my priorities on expanding the business. I'd deliberately sidestepped issues involving internal efficiencies. Bill, I had hoped, would be perfect for this part of the job. And he mostly was.

As much as I liked Bill, personally, I grew increasingly concerned that he wasn't moving far enough or fast enough to build the organization. He was focusing too much on the low hanging fruit and not enough on the tougher integration and rationalization issues. Also, when he hit roadblocks, he was often too soft and conciliatory.

When I met with him, I could tell he was feeling the stress. "Even when I get these guys in Europe together to hash things out," Bill confided, "the only result is a marathon debate, where everyone challenges everyone else on the tiniest of issues. I had thought when I arrived that I could crack the whip and tell them what to do. But I learned after my first few months that this would be impossible. They don't know me, and I don't know them well enough, either. They have their own dynamic written in a code I cannot seem to crack."

I nodded, understanding Bill's problem only too well.

He frowned. "If a tornado swept our country managers into the stratosphere during a meeting, they'd spend the rest of the day arguing over the wind velocity instead of figuring out how to get free. They seem to think they've accomplished something just by arguing, even when no decisions are made."

More Replacements

As Bill neared the end of his four-year tenure, he grew increasingly weary of turnover among key leaders he wanted to retain, and also of what he viewed as European arrogance and intransigence among the leaders he wouldn't mind losing. He finally decided it was time to crack some heads together. His plan was to fire some of the most strident country GMs, replacing them with Americans. When he called to tell me this, I asked for a list of replacements. He replied that it was still early and that he'd present his recommendations later.

CHAPTER

20

LOCALIZATION AND LEADERS

"DAVID, YOUR EYES SEEM A BIT GLAZED OVER. SHOULD WE TAKE A BREAK?" Jacques asked.

"No. I'm okay."

"Well, maybe I should summarize my assessment of Snack Foods up to this point."

I nodded in agreement.

"By the early 1990s, Snack Foods had recognized the need to move from an export orientation to a more international business operation. I remember helping you establish the first manufacturing plant in Lyon. Snack Foods sent in the Americans to set up shop. Most were chosen because they knew the AFG system back home and embraced the *Snack Foods Way*. What you call *The Way* had been critical to the company's success, *n'est pas vrai?*"

"Correct." I set my pen down.

"So it was the job of these American expatriates, many from operations and production, to set up a largely identical system in Europe. These managers had worked in the United States with other American employees and spoke only English fluently."

"Yes. Of course."

Jacques paused for a moment. "Some local employees had to be hired, and I assisted you with locating translators for job interviews and recommending recruitment firms. If I recall correctly, deciding what type of local leaders should be chosen was a dilemma for you. On the one hand, you wanted to recruit local managers who understood the local markets and local ways of doing business. On the other hand, you needed to hire people who would conform to the *Snack Foods Way* and listen to directions or follow orders without saying, 'No, no. This is *not* the way it is done in France.' So, what did you end up with? 'Yes men,' no?"

I nodded. "Yes, I guess that is what we got."

Jacques shook his head but looked at me with sympathy. "These local leaders could follow your orders, but when you needed real insights into how to penetrate the local market, you found them lacking. They did not proactively propose modifications to your products, your marketing, or your packaging."

Jacques continued, "As you and your colleagues began adapting to local tastes, you started to enjoy more success. But your first crop of local managers proved unsatisfactory in helping you to regionalize the products and marketing strategies. They were doers instead of thinkers or good leaders."

"That's right," I said.

"In response, you recruited a second crop of local leaders who really knew the local markets and had proven track records. Beginning in the late 1990s, you switched approaches and began to recruit high-caliber local leaders. Although unhappy about it, you were even willing to pay a premium to lure talent away from the local companies. But with the talent came some strong opinions and more in-fighting than you were used to or prepared to accept. Isn't this correct?"

I nodded again.

"Then, I think it was in December 2000, when Bill announced his resignation from the firm."

"Yes, he told me he was tired of work in general, but also of the in-fighting across Europe. He said he was ready to retire and go back home to spend time with his wife and grandchildren. I could understand. Bill recommended as his replacement Nicolas Peeters, a Belgian. I think you know Nicolas, because we turned to him when we set up Belgium as a stand-alone subsidiary in 1993. We were sorry to have to pull Belgium and The Netherlands from your territory that year. You told us at the time that you understood. I hope you still do."

Jacques nodded his agreement. "All is forgiven."

Still, I could sense that he still harbored some resentment that I hadn't let our previous understanding of the porous boundaries of France and Switzerland continue in perpetuity. I continued, "In December 2000, Nicolas was the European head of marketing and sales. At this time, the choice of a European was considered a big deal, both within Snack Foods and the industry overall. Within AFG at that time, every region was run by an American. Promoting a local over an expat was controversial. It was also seen as a progressive move compared with AFG's American competitors, all of which relied on U.S. expats to run their European headquarters."

"If I remember correctly, you were a bit reluctant but ultimately agreed."

"Jacques, you remember correctly because we had a couple of long conversations about it. But the view at the time was that because sales were continuing to grow for us in Europe, and Nicolas was seen as a big part of Europe's success, his promotion made sense. I liked Nicolas and knew him to be honest, hard-working, and very smart. He was not a 'yes man' and could more than stand his ground. He also knew the industry, after 25 years in snack foods with a couple of different companies before us. Despite my worry that he had worked for our company for only five years, I decided to give him the job. It was a good decision."

Hans was genuinely curious. "So how did he do?"

"Nicolas brought a new energy to Snack Foods Europe. He also helped boost the morale of many of the country GMs. The next three years witnessed solid successes in Snack Foods' performance in Europe. Sales growth seemed back on track, surpassing 20 percent every year.

"But," I added, "none of the stream-lining and housecleaning started by Bill ever materialized. Quite the opposite. Nicolas undertook a slow and steady process of replacing U.S. expats with locals when the expats returned home, and he allowed the locals to adapt not just products, formulations, and packaging to their home markets but also IT, financial, and HR systems to fit their unique needs. The new managers loved and embraced this localization. For eight years, Nicolas fostered this localization with great results."

Anjanette interjected, "You say, 'great results,' but I hear something else in your voice."

"No. Nicolas delivered great results. In fact, I replicated the general pattern that occurred in Snack Foods Europe in our other international regions within Snack Foods. I started replacing many of the expats with high quality local leaders in Asia and Latin America, which we had entered in 1994 and 1995 respectively. In addition, our general pattern of localization opened the floodgates in other AFG overseas affiliates around the world, even outside Snack Foods. In 2001, of AFG's 20 major country operations overseas, non-U.S. nationals headed a total of eleven. With the exception of Europe, the regional heads were all American. The foreign affiliates enjoyed one success after another, as local managers pushed the needed localization.

"By 2001, nearly 55 percent of Snack Food's products sold in Europe were completely or partially unique to Europe, with different formulations, packaging and/or variations of U.S. ingredients. In Asia, the number was 38 percent, and in Latin America it was 29 percent."

CHAPTER
21

THE DEEP STRUGGLE

HANS MOVED BACK TO THE FRONT OF OUR GROUP. "THIS BRINGS US TO THE fourth phase of development—localization. It is the most complicated phase and has a few moving parts, so bear with me as I try to describe what we have seen." He once again put the basic model on the screen (see Figure 21-1).

Stages on the Path of Globalization

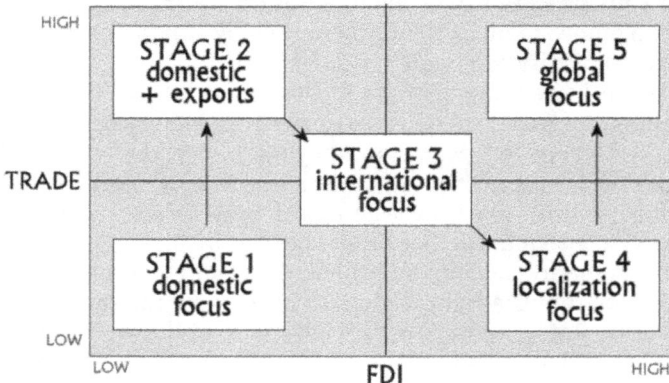

"At this stage firms have finally figured out that they need local leaders who know and understand the local markets and will push to make adjustments, adaptations, and even wholesale innovations in order to penetrate the market."

"Okay, I'm with you. This is where we were in 2001."

"These strong-minded leaders pushed for a variety of changes. The changes could have been in products, processes, or management style. In isolation and early on, these changes seemed to make sense. However, over time, you discovered that you now had perhaps eight different IT platforms and twelve financial systems, five different job-grading schemes, and so on. And the costs of these differences started to add up. At some point, the costs became large enough that they could not be ignored. Not only were there cost issues, but the many fiefdoms that were taking root also started to put Snack Foods' brands and values at risk. Then someone at headquarters noticed and decided that some duplications needed to be eliminated, some manufacturing facilities rationalized, and some branding policies standardized. Am I correct?"

I winced. That touched a raw nerve.

Hans moved on quickly. "This brings us to the fifth stage of development. Many firms struggle enormously at this stage. One reason is that the strong-minded local executives the company put in place to produce these differences, these local responses, typically resist the harmonization or integration—or what most of them see as wrongheaded centralization efforts. It's understandable they resist."

Hans was off the mark here and I started to say something, but he politely gave me no chance.

"I did not say that they are correct in resisting. I said it is understandable why they do this. After all, from their perspective, the growth just before this point was because they insisted on and implemented the adaptations, innovations, and the responses to local needs. And their experiences testify that they were correct. Because they are not 'yes men' they push back. Openly at first. I hope you realize that if their arguments are not well received, often their efforts at resistance go underground and they say, 'yes,' to your face regarding the integration efforts but then they tell their people to ignore them or to only superficially support them."

"Okay, go on." Irritation made my voice gruff.

"Often those in senior positions at headquarters are the ones who were first sent out years ago to open up operations. Now, years later, when they see this resistance to integration, they often view the resisters as examples of the 'rigid, locally focused, pain in the butt' leaders that they purposely did not hire way back when as they were setting up the new operations. As a consequence, they often take this insurrection as evidence that they were right and decide the leaders who cannot see, embrace, and live *The Way* were not the right leaders to hire or, for that matter, retain. To ensure that the integration goes forward, some of these strong-minded local leaders are encouraged to retire early or maybe even a few are fired. Most often they are replaced by loyal soldiers from the mother ship."

"I think that is an unfair phrase. The 'mother ship,' really?" My eyebrows furrowed.

"Perhaps you are right, but if you look at it from the perspective of the local leaders in the field, it is not an unfair or exaggerated term. From their perspective they have done exactly what they were hired to do. They made the changes necessary to more aggressively penetrate the market, but now what they did is being undone by captains sitting in fancy chairs and offices who, they believe, have no real idea what is going on in the trenches and who send in drones from the mother ship to replace them all so they can go backward and undo all the hard-fought progress. The cries for integration and standardization are a huge threat to drivers of their success."

"Yes, but just because they see it that way, doesn't mean it is accurate," I replied.

Jacques spoke up. "David, you are taking this personally. What Hans is describing is a general pattern. We have talked with many managers in this position. These non-home-country managers, whether the home country of the company is the U.S., France, Germany, or Japan, too often believe that they are not sufficiently rewarded or that their ideas aren't respected. When they see like-minded colleagues replaced by new expats from the home country, it just reaffirms to them that there is a glass ceiling when it comes to promotions for regional roles or positions at the corporate level."

Hans stepped in again. "If you are a foreign manager and think you have some potential, you start to wonder about your future in a company that focuses on the *Corporate Way* and just keeps sending in expats from the mother ship. The companies do this while ignoring the contributions of smart and dedicated local leaders. As a consequence, the best local leaders start leaving. This often leads the expats to say, 'See, I told you we could not count on these local managers to stay loyal.' This then leads to even more expats being sent in or at least it leads to no local leaders moving into important decision-making roles. Not only this, but their absence and the rotation of expats every three years starts to slow sales and complicate relationships, both within the foreign country and between the affiliate and headquarters. This further entrenches the leaders back home to rely on known and trusted leaders to turn things around. These leaders are inevitably from the mother ship. Not knowing the local market and not being able to tap into it via high quality local managers further hurts performance. Soon you can have a vicious cycle."

Jacques jumped in again. "To put this in context, retaining foreign executives has been a challenge not only for American companies, but for European and Asian companies, especially the Japanese."

"Really?"

"You should be grateful that AFG is not a Japanese company, *mon ami*. You would find it almost impossible to recruit top-tier talent for your overseas management teams. I have a good friend, a professor at a famous international business school just down the road in Lausanne, and he tells me that his graduating MBA students view a job with a Japanese firm merely as a springboard. None believe that a non-Japanese can become a senior global executive. Look what happened to the poor British fellow who was made CEO of Olympus."

"What happened?"

"He was fired the first time he raised a thorny issue."

Fired? I could relate to that.

"My professor friend says that his students talk about the 'bamboo ceiling,' the notion that if you are not Japanese, you can go only so far in your career with a Japanese company. Personally, I can relate to this as I am half Japanese."

Jacques's words clicked in my mind. I frowned. "Are you implying that Snack Foods is biased against non-Americans?"

"Yes. Indeed, I am."

"I can't believe you would say that. You know I have friends from all over the world. We just haven't found locals who are both loyal team players and good managers."

Jacques lifted his coffee cup and held it up as if he was proud of what he had said.

I was upset. After all our years of friendship, how could he suggest that I would deny people entrance to the ranks of upper management just because they were not Americans?

"I'm not suggesting that you and your executive team are *deliberately* biased," he said. "Everyone has prejudices and biases. You have spent enough time here to know that even the neutral Swiss are not without fault in this respect. Of course in Switzerland we believe that the best tennis player in the history of the world is Roger Federer."

"You can say that again." I stared at the crackling fire warming the chalet.

It's a Matter of Trust

"It is only natural that you trust the people you know, and you know best those people who are close to you," Jacques said. "If you work in a French company, those people will most naturally be French. If you work in an American company, those people will be American. You and your colleagues have worked together, played together, and overcome adversity together for years and years. You have formed relationships and cemented the kinds of loyalties that you see among soldiers who have fought in combat together."

He looked right at me and added, "You would never say, 'Pierre is French so I'm not going to promote him to Vice President of Marketing.' No. It's about promoting Joe, who you've known for twenty years, because you know him, like him, and trust him. Also, there is no question that Joe is familiar with and devoted to what you call the *Snack Foods Way*."

I gazed back at Jacques.

He shrugged. Truce. "Your American colleague is a member of your network. Pierre is an outsider. Someone brought in to help the company penetrate local markets. Not someone who was recruited to work in St. Louis and be part of the core family."

"That's not . . . " I was about to say that Jacques was completely off base, but I realized that he might actually have a good point. I couldn't think of a single non-American executive at corporate. I motioned for him to continue.

He nodded. "This new cadre of leaders did what you hired them to do. They made many modifications, adaptations, and even some innovations. And sales grew. Over time, these differences added up, and the costs of different systems and platforms were too big to ignore. When you tried to integrate them, or should I say when your CEO pushed you to integrate them, the strong-willed local leaders that you'd hired *resisted*. After all, what had made them successful was adapting things to local markets, not making things the same around the world. They do what most strong-willed talented leaders do. They acted according to what they thought was right and ignored what they believed to be wrong-headed. And I might add, they also saw integration as a threat to their power. Wouldn't you?"

Jacques continued, "I am merely repeating the perspective of these managers. I make no judgments. These facts are clear, are they not? These people were convinced their expertise and efforts were unappreciated. Many were ready to leave, but they just needed a good reason."

"And this reason came between 2000 and 2002," he said, "when a down economy made you look closely at your costs. You discovered that over more than a decade of localization, which drove sales, you had built up a patchwork of different and sometimes incompatible systems and small and inefficient factories. You then logically pushed for rationalization, consolidation, and integration. This is why they began leaving in droves. When you moved to consolidate, shut down factories, and rationalize product lines, it provided the final evidence that their futures were limited and that Snack Foods would never *really* succeed overseas."

I shook my head, remembering how they sabotaged my globalization efforts and made me look like a dupe. Now they might even cost me my job and reputation.

CHAPTER

22

QUIET INSURRECTION

HEARING ABOUT THIS FINAL PHASE WAS THE TOUGHEST. THE INCIDENTS THAT paralleled the framework under discussion were so recent, I felt I could almost touch them.

Beginning with the recession of 2000 and the downward acceleration caused by the terrorist attacks of September 11, 2001, AFG started looking closely at its worldwide costs and structures. In February 2002, Ron Walker, AFG's CEO, asked all division presidents to provide a summary of the different control systems they were using around the world. We were given four weeks to prepare our reports.

I received the news with apprehension, since requests like this often presaged corporate "streamlining." I also knew the request was not without merit. Because of all the localization that had become vital to our success, Snack Foods had been perhaps more haphazard than other divisions in developing common systems and practices.

Just as Hans had described, after a comprehensive review, we discovered that in the time that I had been running the worldwide Snack Food division, it had slowly and almost imperceptibly ballooned through some acquisitions and general localization into a vast array of different and sometimes incompatible systems:

- twelve different financial and accounting systems
- ten major IT systems
- eighteen different performance appraisal systems
- no standardized succession planning system
- no coordinated executive development or training system
- six different quality control systems
- no integrated purchasing system across countries or regions

Globally, Snack Foods also had four different brands of its top-selling chocolate chip cookie (with slightly different formulations), six different cracker brands (two of which used the same recipe), and two brands of the same mixed nuts fighting for shelf space. All of this duplication was wasting a lot of money and in some cases confusing customers.

Bring in the Consultants

In an effort to pre-empt Ron's follow-up questions, I quietly retained one of the Big Four accounting firms to do a quick-and-dirty assessment of the cost implications of this duplication. Ten days later—just one day before my report was due—the accountants concluded that the duplication of production facilities, conflict in brands and distribution, and missed opportunities to reduce costs through consolidated purchases were adding between 18 and 30 percent to Snack Foods' fixed costs and 12 to 16 percent to the variable costs of the production of our cookies, crackers, and so on. The accountants estimated consolidation could save the Snack Foods Division between $66 million and $96 million per year on $1.79 billion in revenues. The biggest area for potential gains was international operations. As a caveat to their report, the accountants added:

We point out that, per your mandate, this review represents a tentative high-level assessment of the opportunities for cost savings. Additional research and testing are necessary to clarify and solidify these numbers. With additional clarity, the estimates may be adjusted upward or downward.

I decided not to share these numbers with Ron. If I did, I would be expected to *do something* about them, and I didn't know if I had the stomach for major factory shutdowns and consolidation. Courage aside, I wondered whether it would even be cost-effective, particularly in Europe. It would cost a lot to undertake shutdowns in Europe, not only in terms of direct costs for layoffs and factory restructuring, but also in terms of management time and attention, particularly in dealing with unions, regulatory authorities, and other powerful local stakeholders. Quite frankly, I wasn't sure that Ron would appreciate a complicated and nuanced cost versus benefits dialogue. He might force shutdowns as a matter of course.

In my report to Ron, I did identify a number of redundancies, indicating that additional research would be conducted to determine the "precise costs of these redundancies." In response, Ron directed me to provide

these costing details and my recommendations, with an action plan, within another 90 days.

I went back to the accountants with the charge of tightening the numbers. I gave them 45 days to complete the task. I instructed them to not
only focus on achieving cost savings by eliminating redundancies but, also,
to calculate the one-time costs associated with layoffs, factory closings,
and other actions. Then I called another group of consultants to perform
a broader review of Snack Foods' worldwide operations with an emphasis
on how we structured our global activities. The consultants were given 30
days to complete their work.

I received their report on April 5, 2002. After giving it a thorough
review, I came back to several paragraphs in the Executive Summary:

> *Your transition into and the nature of borderless global com-*
> *petition are marked by the re-emergence of two dynamics*
> *that played leading but sequential roles in the export and in-*
> *ternationalization stages of your growth.*

> *In the export stage of your early international growth, the*
> *economies of scale and benefits of standardization pushed*
> *you to focus on making products one way at home, and then*
> *selling them exactly the same way around the world.*

> *In the internalization stage of your growth, the differences*
> *across regions and countries pushed you to begin modifying*
> *and adapting to local differences.*

> *In the global stage of your growth, both forces—the forces for*
> *global integration and for local adaptation—simultaneously*
> *hold sway.*

The consultants stressed that Snack Foods would have to struggle
with, and eventually master, a complex process of determining which
things to globally integrate, which things to locally differentiate, and which
activities and products to blend with a bit of both. They emphasized that a
global strategy does *not* mean doing everything the same way around the
world. It also does *not* mean that the company should "think global and
act local." Instead, it meant that Snack Foods would need to:
- globally integrate and standardize some activities in thought
and action;
- locally differentiate other activities in thought and action; and
- create global-local hybrids for still other activities.

Although I appreciated the report's strategic insights, it was long on
dialogue but short on details of *what* should actually be done. Which activities should be globalized and controlled out of St. Louis? Which control
systems should continue to be controlled by local subsidiaries? Which lo-

cal brands should be pushed out of the way for global brands, and which factories should be shut down? And what aspects, if any, of *The Way* would need to be updated? The devil was always in the details. The recommendation that senior Snack Foods managers simultaneously think in multi-directions was fine in theory, but no one knew the implications if this theory were to be applied to the real world.

The consultant's report said that Snack Foods needed a process to achieve greater rationalization. No doubt. I assumed the consulting firm wanted another contract so it could develop this process and then help implement it. They weren't going to get it.

The Accountants' Final Report

Three weeks after I received the consultants' report, I met with the accountants to review their findings. They concluded that their earlier preliminary review was directionally correct, but they added several modifications. Cost savings was increased to a range of $73 million to $127 million annually. Non-recurring costs associated with layoffs, plant closures, and other changes would range from a low of $82 million to a high of more than $200 million, depending on scope and timing. The net non-recurring numbers included variables such as the layoffs, revenues generated by the sale of properties, tax implications, and other factors. Notably, they did *not* assess the impact of the changes on the brands, channels, or supplier relationships.

The accountants were adamant in pointing out that all cost assessments were dependent on location. For example, they indicated that laying off employees in Denmark in 2002 could cost the company the equivalent of more than four years' salary per employee in redundancy penalties. In Switzerland, such penalties represented just a few month's work per employee.

Regardless of location, the accountants said it was impossible to entirely de-couple variable and fixed costs, but that they could use powerful algorithms to help Snack Foods weigh the many decisions required to streamline its operations globally. Of course they would charge us additional money for this work.

I knew that algorithms and tentative reports from consultants and accountants would not be enough to satisfy Ron Walker. The clock was ticking and I worried that Ron was so driven by short-term pressures to pump up the firm's stock price that he was determined to shutter plants and rationalize operations. I feared he'd overlook the true cost-benefit tradeoffs. My only source of solace was the fact that the other three divisional heads were probably facing the same challenges I was.

The Report to the CEO

In my final report to Ron, I wrote in part:

Based on our preliminary review, we have estimated that rationalizing our operations could save approximately $75 million per year. However, this savings would come with substantial one-time costs that could go as high as $200 million. It is impossible to be more precise because there are too many variables to consider in such a short time. Nevertheless, we estimate it will take 3-5 years before the annual savings of rationalization will exceed the one-time charges.

Moving forward will require a great deal of study to ensure that disruptions are minimized and cost savings are optimized. We are confident this can be done, but care is in order.

We recommend moving forward with a plan to globally align five key activities: purchasing, supply chain management, finance, HR and branding. We do not recommend proceeding beyond this until we have a better sense of where AFG is moving on corporate-level systems and practices.

I hedged a little on the cost savings associated with rationalization, presenting numbers to Ron that were a bit more conservative than the accountants' numbers. I wasn't about to commit to numbers that not even the accountants could justify. Also, I wanted to indicate that I would support change, but that I was cautious about moving forward.

I later learned that my report was directionally similar to those of the other division GMs. I benefited from reasonably good data from the accountants, plus additional strategic insights from the consultants. Because of this, my recommendations went further than the suggestions made by my peers. Still, I would be the first to admit that my report lacked detail.

The CEO's Response

Ron Walker had started with AFG in 1975 and had spent his entire career in the U.S. Though he'd traveled extensively, he didn't have any experience as an expatriate. I also knew that his personal interest was in the U.S. and not in international markets. Ron was keenly focused on bottom-line performance and the stock price. He wasn't someone who micro-managed, which was a blessing. He knew very little about effective globalization, so I was relieved by his reaction to my presentation. He seemed genuinely pleased with my report, and he particularly liked my efforts at quantifying savings. Yes, he was concerned about the one-time costs since we couldn't yet accurately estimate them. He gave me the green light to proceed with global rationalization, and he gave me three years to make it pay off. Although not a math major in university, I knew that $200 million in one-time costs would take more than three years to pay off if our savings were less than $75 million per year. It seemed I had no choice but to be more aggressive on our rationalization efforts than I would have liked.

After reviewing each of the divisional reports, Ron organized a meeting with the four GMs. As part of his presentation he said,

> *Snack Foods seems to be the furthest along in their thinking, so I would like them to take a one-year lead in their efforts to globally rationalize operations. I've asked David to keep me—and through me, each of you— apprised of both his progress and his education. He'll send me quarterly updates. In the meantime, I want those of you running the other three divisions to keep your powder dry. A year from now you may be fighting the same battle David will soon be fighting.*

CHAPTER

23

GLOBALIZATION 2.0

I WASN'T SURE WHAT TO THINK AFTER RON SINGLED OUT SNACK FOODS. IT was either his stamp of approval or a set-up for failure. Either way, I had no choice but to get down to business. I appointed Cameron Lafferty to a newly created position of Director of Global Operations. His job was to recommend a globalization action plan by end of 2002, less than six months away.

Lafferty had joined AFG straight out of college, and now at age 56, he had managerial experience in all four divisions. He also had considerable international experience; he'd run the international division for Bakery out of St. Louis and completed short-term assignments in Toronto, London, Singapore, and Melbourne. I viewed him as mature and politically savvy.

While I relied on Lafferty to take the lead, I made sure I was kept up to date. We met every two weeks over the next few months to review progress and bounce ideas around. On December 8, Lafferty presented me with a draft of his globalization plan for Snack Foods. After suggesting a few modifications, I called a global conference of Snack Foods' senior leaders to announce the plan. The meeting was held December 20, 2002 in St. Louis.

The Plan

After reviewing some of our research and discussing the imperatives placed on us by Ron Walker, I declared to the 64 senior Snack Foods people in attendance that we would need to shutter 20 percent of our plants around the world and that within two years each country would have to carry a minimum of 50 percent of the same standardized Snack Foods products. I didn't provide more details. I didn't mention which plants would be closed and which common products would be sold in every market. I didn't mention which processes would be used or how, when, and where.

Though I had pre-worked most of the details of plant closings and product line rationalizations, I didn't want to jump the gun and overlook possible areas of strength or competitive realities that might have been hidden from head office. I also wanted to involve the senior management group in the discussions and allow the country GMs and other functional heads to fight for solutions that made the most sense. I gave them 25 days to come back with their best ideas. I figured if they were smart, they would not only do their homework but would also sit down with other units to work out solutions that could be mutually beneficial. If they were too dumb or arrogant to figure this out or work out effective plans, well, so be it. Their fate would be sealed.

What I didn't know at the time was that my announcement infuriated some of the local managers heading our big overseas affiliates, especially since they hadn't been involved in any of the build-up discussions. I found out later that after our December 20 meeting, these same country general managers had met at a local restaurant to discuss their frustrations and devise a response. Most of them vowed to ignore the substance of the initiative while making it *seem* they were supportive. By the time their reports were due on January 17, only two of the units, the affiliates in Brazil and Singapore, had proposed any meaningful rationalization plans. The plans from the other units were vague and vacuous.

I was done waiting. On January 24, I called the group back together and announced the closing of plants in twelve countries. I also presented a list of ten Snack Foods products that every affiliate *must* carry, unadulterated or modified, by the end of 2003. I then presented sales targets in chart form that would be applied for purposes of personal performance bonuses in 2003 and 2004. Finally, I announced the "resignations" of six of my most obstinate country General Managers. I had planned to do this for some time but had waited for the January 24 meeting as a way to signal to the organization that I meant business. None of the six were in attendance. They'd been told of their terminations the day before in conference calls with me.

I asked at the end of my presentation if there were any questions. Not a single hand was raised.

Lessons from Korea

Little did I know the insurrection that had begun in December continued to simmer. I knew many of the GMs weren't happy. I thought with the departure of the gang of six sour GMs, things would slowly calm down and life would return to normal. I was wrong.

The quiet insurrection lasted another two years before I got wind of it. On one of my regular overseas excursions, I toured our South Korean factory near Seoul. At the end of the day, managers Young-soo Kim and Hyun-jun Jeong invited me to their favorite restaurant to sample Korea's famous barbecue meats. I'm not a big meat eater, but I thought it would be impolite to decline. Young-soo said the food at the restaurant was excellent, more authentically Korean than the fare at my hotel.

Once we were seated and the waitress had brought a bottle of Korea's famous distilled liquor, Soju, I noted a curious custom. Hyun-jun took the Soju bottle with both hands and filled the shot glasses, offering them to each of us with both hands. I declined. I don't drink. This seemed to surprise, even stun, my Korean friends. After a moment of embarrassed silence, Hyun-jun then held his glass with two hands while Young-soo, his boss, filled it using just one hand to grasp the bottle. When I asked about this ritual, Young-soo told me using two hands to accept and offer food and drink during meals was a traditional sign of respect. When serving one's superior, it was considered respectful to hold the bottle or pitcher with both hands.

I was about to ask if this custom was universally observed when out of the corner of my eye I spotted Snack Foods' South Korean GM, Gun-woo Park, leaving the restaurant in the company of some businessmen. I hadn't noticed he was in the restaurant. When I asked my companions if Mr. Park frequented the restaurant, they exchanged quick glances, and Hyun-jun muttered something about a "lack of respect" under his breath.

I let the matter drop, but within forty minutes, both men were so well lubricated with Soju that they began speaking *very* candidly about Mr. Park and the Seoul corporate office. I was ready to excuse myself, since I wasn't in the mood for Machiavellian maneuvering among lower-level managers, when Young-soo addressed me directly. "Mr. Anderson, I have wanted for some time to make you aware of some issues taking place here, but I said nothing because it wasn't my place. Now that I've gotten to know you better, I see that you are an honest and intelligent man, so I feel the need to speak out. You should know that many of your office's directives are being ignored or even undermined by the local management at the behest of Mr. Park."

"What? Undermined how?" I tried not to let the alarm ringing in my head show on my face.

Young-soo glanced at his companion and then back at me. "For some time, Mr. Jeong and I have been discreetly instructed to disregard some policies and processes ordered by your office in St. Louis and to follow instructions only from Mr. Park's office. I wasn't aware that we were contradicting St. Louis until recently, but we've been told to withhold timely data on costs and instead report very confusing data that would require an army of accountants at HQ to decipher. Our salespeople have also been instructed to push the local brands over the global brands. By doing this, we believe Mr. Park hopes that an increase in sales of local brands will make us safe from consolidation. It would also prove to HQ that its efforts to globalize the products are a mistake."

I stared at him in disbelief. "What else can you tell me?"

"Some of the local managers believe you are prejudiced against anyone who is not an American," said Hyun-yung. "This is obvious, they say, because no Koreans have been promoted to run regions or take jobs at headquarters. Also, they say that you are very arrogant because you would not listen to us when you forced us to close one of our two plants here in Korea. Because of this our revenues have dropped by 35 percent, causing our sales people to suffer huge stresses. While Snack Foods might have saved some costs, we lost a lot of face with our customers. We were forced to cancel many products our customers loved and promote only American products. Also, the longer global supply chains you have promoted mean more stock-outs and less harmonious relations. In response, we have quietly added back most of the local Korean products we initially canceled. We buried the results in our sales numbers by consolidating the categories of products in our reports. We are very sorry to be reporting this to you."

I managed to check my anger, for the moment, and actively listen to what my companions had to say, asking only a handful of additional, albeit terse questions. When I was satisfied that they had no more information to impart, I thanked them for their insights and promised that their loyalty would not be forgotten. I returned to my hotel to phone Lafferty, asking him to find evidence of what the Koreans told me.

In the weeks ahead, Lafferty not only confirmed what was happening in South Korea, but also discovered the insurrection had taken hold in other large affiliates across the globe, especially France, Italy, Mexico and India. Not only were they hiding local products, they were often producing them through sub-contractors and creatively burying the costs.

A Futile Defense

Once their activities were exposed, the insubordinate country managers vigorously defended their actions with data showing that the localization campaigns had actually fueled successes in their countries, and that these successes were collectively responsible for Snack Foods' global growth (as sales were mostly flat in the U.S. and had been for nearly a decade). These local leaders argued that the *Snack Foods Way* of doing business did not resonate well with them or their employees, who were uncomfortable with some of our values and approaches, such as working out disagreements quickly and debating decisions publicly, which seemed quintessentially American.

Then it hit me. These were *exactly* the type of arrogant, self-centered, non-team players I had refused to hire when I set up Snack Foods' first international affiliate in France. Despite our best efforts to screen out the Pierre Ovrards of the world, some of them had infiltrated our overseas operations and tried to pull a fast one. Insubordination wouldn't be tolerated. Not for a second. If these managers had reservations about the global initiative, they should have spoken their minds at the first opportunity instead of behaving like second-string Sun Tzu's who treated me like an enemy. I resented being cast as someone to be appeased and duped.

In my view, these were serious ethical breaches and as soon as I had the confirmation from Lafferty, I knew I had to take swift action. I confronted the problem head on and, within 24 hours, fired four rebel country GMs, including Gun-woo Park from Korea, and 24 hours after that I fired 22 of their deputies. I also ordered a thorough review of our financial oversight procedures and asked my CFO to look into replacing the local auditors. To this day, it is still referred to as the "great purge" at Snack Foods.

Other Rebels at Play

I realized that the rebel activities were likely not limited to these four countries. The GMs in other countries, while perhaps not acting in ways that warranted termination, were almost certainly dragging their feet in more subtle yet still worrisome ways. With a few exceptions, our biggest resisters seemed to be located in our largest affiliates. I directed Lafferty to meet with as many of these GMs and other senior overseas executives as possible. I wanted to know more and understand what we were up against.

In his follow-up report, Lafferty singled out Gustavo Santos as a representative example of the "disgruntled, overseas executive." When Lafferty spoke with him, Santos was the deputy CEO of Snack Foods' Brazilian affiliate. Santos' business unit employed 1,800 people and included a manufacturing facility in Sao Paulo Brazil.

During an earlier discussion with Santos, Lafferty had mentioned to him that we would be traveling to Brazil and meeting with his American boss, the regional VP, two weeks later. Santos' face turned bright red. He asked, "Could you please ask him how he thinks I'm doing?"

Lafferty replied, "Why don't you ask him yourself?"

"I always ask him that question," said Santos. "And he always says the same thing. 'You are doing fine.' I don't believe him. It isn't that I'm doing badly, but he doesn't open up to me. He doesn't tell me anything."

"We hired you to represent the global values of the firm," said Lafferty. "And one of those values is 'Don't be afraid to say what you mean and mean what you say.' How long have you worked for us?"

"I've been with the company for ten years," replied Santos. "In fact, I'm the most senior Brazilian here. But I don't know how effective I really am. I attend all the senior meetings, but they are all conducted in English and sometimes the speed of conversation is so fast, I can barely keep up. So I don't say much and the regional leaders don't ask me anything."

"Where do you go from here, career-wise? What are your future leadership prospects at Snack Foods?"

Santos said, "I have nowhere to go. My career has reached its zenith. While I have learned to speak reasonable English, it doesn't seem to matter. The American executives won't let me into their circle because I am not one of them. And I never will be. To be honest, I got this far only because I pretend to be a humble servant. If I were to start agitating for more control in Brazil, it wouldn't be tolerated. This is the end of the line for me."

Within a month, Santos resigned. Soon, many of the rabble-rousing managers with whom Lafferty met in other countries also tendered their resignations.

More Departures

At the time, I believed these departures reinforced my view that foreign nationals didn't have the same loyalty to the company as Americans. They were overpaid, proud, and not keen on working as a team. They were not the kind of people Snack Foods could rely on in the long run.

I recalled the letter Hans had sent to the regional head when he resigned as the GM for Snack Foods in Germany; the letter was forwarded to me.

> *The senior executives in St. Louis just don't get it. They think that if you cannot mold your thinking and career aspirations to theirs that you are disloyal and selfish. I'm moving on because I will never be accepted as an equal. The job (a regional SVP in a German competitor) that I am leaving for is in my view a natural progression. However, if I had I stayed in this company I would never have been promoted to such a position. No one but an American has ever held that job, and no one but an American ever will.*

> *Maybe I'm not good enough, but I lived in America for over three years and speak the language. I love the country and the culture. If someone like me cannot be considered for a global role, I'm not sure who could be.*

When I called the European regional head to better understand what was going on, he replied with a very different interpretation of Hans's reasons for leaving:

> *Hans doesn't understand. We had high hopes for him as GM in Germany. Because he's spent time in America, he could have performed a vital function and could have been an important link between HQ and the affiliate. We're disappointed in Hans, considering our investment in him. Given his interest in America, we were surprised that he so easily focused on money and a promotion and would leave us. We will be careful to avoid this mistake again.*

What I didn't realize at the time was that within a year, Hans would be working for my good friend Jacques. When I pressed Jacques about this, he replied, "My dear David, I would never have stolen Hans directly from you. This is not what friends do. But when I knew he was in play, I went after him. Hiring him from your German competitor was something I think you should thank me for."

Bringing in the Americans

As I recalled, on the recommendation of Lafferty and with my endorsement, Snack Foods began systematically replacing many of these senior local executives with American expatriates. No more people were fired. Some were transferred; others left for better opportunities.

While there had been many benefits from the years of localization, there had also been costs. We needed to take those costs out of the system. Too many local leaders had worked secretly to slow the rationalization efforts or even sabotage them, and it was now clear to me that few locals could be trusted with the challenging task of global integration. Only leaders who had spent significant time in the head office could be trusted to be loyal over their entire careers, remaining committed to the *Snack Foods Way* and the values and approaches that had made our company great.

CHAPTER

24

HIT BY CRISIS

DESPITE THE ANNOYANCE AND STRESS THAT ACCOMPANIED THE DEPARTURE of the insurrectionists, I took some solace from the knowledge that their departures spared us some potentially unpleasant confrontations. But my stay at this mental oasis was short-lived. Over the next few years, Snack Foods endured an alarming and unwanted exodus of bright and talented local managers in all countries with overseas operations. Resignations poured in from everywhere: Denmark, South Africa, France, India, Germany, Italy, the Netherlands, Brazil, Spain, Korea, Switzerland, China, Mexico, even the U.K. By spring 2010, one-third of the mid-level managers had quit

As these locals left the company, I received copies of resignation letters that referenced the same list of grievances and frustrations. Most of the managers pointed out that they'd made much-needed modifications and adjustments to our original line of products and even developed new products to better fit the markets. They complained that regardless of the results their diligent efforts produced, they were consistently passed over for significant regional roles and believed they had absolutely no chance of obtaining positions at the global corporate level. They blamed senior management's bias toward Americans over foreign nationals, especially those with less-than-perfect English-language skills, or who expressed values and attitudes that differed from those of Americans. A few radicals even accused me and the Snack Foods executive team of racism or sexism and, in one case, homophobia. I barely knew the manager who made that accusation and had no clue he was gay. Such was the nature of the venom seeping through the organization.

The bottom line? These local leaders thought they were getting a bum deal. They believed their ideas were being ignored and that they would never be promoted with Americans running the show. So, they packed up their offices to pursue jobs at other multinationals or at regional firms run by their own countrymen.

Revenue Weakness

Meanwhile, revenues at Snack Foods were showing signs of weakness. Between 2006 and 2010, U.S. sales revenues had barely budged, rising less than 1 percent. Of course many managers argued that the financial crisis of 2008 and the global recession in 2009 were to blame. However, when you looked at international sales, which represented 34 percent of total revenues, compared with U.S. domestic sales, it was clear that international sales were significantly underperforming. The good news was, compared with AFG's other divisions, Snack Foods was holding its own. We were basically flat in a bad economy.

I saw few connections between these numbers and the wave of recent resignations. If anything, I was inclined to blame stagnant sales on the departing locals. Maybe with them gone, results would pick up. Or maybe not, but at least morale would improve. I had no idea that my leadership of Snack Foods in its global phase of growth was turning into a rout.

Still, I had a growing sense that Americanizing the company's international operations might not have been such a great idea. A closer examination of sales data convinced me that after introducing many American snack food products into large swaths of Europe, Latin America, and Asia, we were too often getting our butt kicked by our biggest rivals. Most of our competitors were growing at between 10 and 20 percent per year in countries such as China and Brazil. Our international market share wasn't growing. In fact, it was shrinking.

This embarrassment could not stand for long if I wanted to keep my job. Something had to be done fast, so in dramatic, take-the-bull-by-the-horns fashion, I scheduled a three-week tour of Europe and Asia to meet with twelve key country managers.

I met dozens of people on my tour. I went out of my way to spend time with a mixture of expatriates and local managers. I kept hearing the same message again and again. Locals complained of U.S. arrogance and missed opportunities to connect with them. Expats complained that the locals, "just didn't get it," when it came to working hard, following through, and getting rid of costly duplication and unnecessary local systems. One newly installed expatriate GM summarized the thinking:

We are working 100 hours per week to increase sales and promote growth, but the locals are lazy, obstructionist and, quite frankly, useless. We can't seem to get them to take our business challenges seriously.

CHAPTER
25

IT'S A MATTER OF BALANCE

"DAVID? WOULD YOU LIKE SOME DESSERT?"

I realized that during lunch my mind had wondered off when the others began discussing their firm's issues that had come up during their phone calls. Jacques gestured at the fresh apple tart his housekeeper had baked that morning.

"Now you need some things, like your IT system, globally integrated," said Jacques, "and some things, like certain flavor formulations, locally adapted. To make this dessert, we all use a round pan. But you have apple pie, and we have tart."

He cut slices for us and set down the knife. "Where was I? Yes, as we were saying before lunch, to figure all this out, you need executives at corporate who have a first-hand knowledge and a deep feel for all of this. You require executives who understand the customers, competitors, employees, regulators, partners, and general communities across all your markets. You cannot do this with only Americans, only French, or only Japanese executives. You need the best and brightest, regardless of passport. You need diversity. Otherwise you will not capture the range of perspective, experience, and expertise necessary for innovative breakthroughs." Jacques leaned forward. "No country or culture has cornered the market on strategy, logistics, supply chain, finance, marketing, or any other area of expertise. If you are going to be innovative and grow, you have no choice but to employ the best human capital wherever you can find it. In short, every multinational must learn to overcome its home-country bias. AFG must become passport blind."

"Makes sense." I took a bite of the tart and decided not to ask for vanilla ice cream.

He frowned. "Snack Foods, and quite frankly all of AFG, is falling farther and farther behind its competitors in this area. You have no senior global executives who are not Americans, whereas my research elves have told me the figures for Nabisco are approximately 16 percent foreign nationals as senior executives, 12 percent for Pepperidge Farms. At Nestlé, foreign nationals fill the majority of senior decision-making roles. In fact I hear that at Nestlé, fluency in a minimum of three languages is now a requirement for promotion to senior management."

"How do you know all of this?" I asked.

"This discussion has focused on Snack Foods and the Japanese so far, but our research project has been quite extensive. Why don't we finish this discussion in the lounge and then hit the slopes?"

CHAPTER
26

A NEW "FORMULATION"

The Example of Japanese Companies

HANS HAD TAKEN HIS PLACE AGAIN AT THE FRONT OF THE ROOM. "AS WE were discussing earlier, many Japanese firms have encountered troubles at what we've labeled 'Stage 5' of globalization." He must have noticed the confused look on my face. "This is the stage at which inputs, manufacturing facilities, support activities, and people are geographically located for optimum results, without preference for particular locations or employee nationalities. Jacques referred to this as passport blind in the location decision.

"In conjunction with several academic friends," Hans continued, "we have reviewed empirical evidence revealing that greater national diversity of top management teams is associated with greater levels of internationalization of their companies *and* with higher global performance. Instead of nurturing local talent that could contribute to their global growth, the top Japanese firms that were followed in these academic studies largely ignored non-Japanese talent. Not surprisingly, many non-Japanese regional managers chose to leave. I believe that Snack Foods is now experiencing the same problem."

I gave him an apologetic smile. "You know this first-hand, don't you Hans?"

Hans shrugged. "Yes, indeed. This problem is not limited to Japanese companies, but it is so pronounced among them that the patterns were easier to recognize, making it quicker to draw accurate conclusions, and develop feasible solutions. But it is happening in companies around the world." He motioned to a new slide filling the screen.

"On average, Japanese multinational corporations or MNCs currently have a lower percentage of top foreign executives than other nations' MNCs. One study examined over 350 European companies, each with more than 1,000 employees and over $500 million in annual revenue, consisting of over 7,000 individual senior executive observations from 2000 to 2005.[1] The study found a significant and growing percentage of non-home nationals among the top executives. The average percentage of foreigners among top executives for Swiss firms was 39 percent, Dutch firms 27 percent, Swedish firms 18 percent, U.K. firms 16 percent, and Finnish firms 10 percent."

He went on. "We knew of no systematic study of the nationalities of Japanese executive teams, so we contracted our own small study. We examined the top ten Japanese firms listed in the *Fortune Global 500* and looked at the nationalities of all the top executives listed in the annual reports for those companies. The companies, in order of rank, were Toyota Motor, Honda Motor, Hitachi, Nissan Motor, Nippon Telegraph & Telephone, Matsushita Electric Industrial, Sony, Toshiba, Nippon Life Insurance, and Nippon Oil.

"On average, each company listed twenty-five top executives. Only 5.5 percent were non-Japanese, and 94.5 percent were Japanese. If you exclude Nissan and Sony from the analysis, both of which had foreigners introduced as the result of significant financial difficulties, then 100 percent of the senior executives were Japanese. None were foreigners. *Not a single one* of the senior executives in these companies were non-Japanese."

"Incredible." I shook my head.

Jacques added, "Remember when we began our discussion this morning, we said the number of Japanese firms on the *Fortune Global 500* list has decreased by 60 percent in the last 15 years? Their global growth has stalled as many of their best leaders outside Japan have pursued better opportunities elsewhere. Who could blame them?"

"Look, we really tried promoting locals at Snack Foods but we just never found the right fit." I shifted my eyes from Jacques to Hans to Anjanette. "What exactly could we have done differently?"

Three Lessons from Our Studies

Hans replied, "There are three major lessons and four concrete actions or 'countermeasures' that we have learned from these studies. First, while there are some unique historical and cultural aspects to Japan and Japanese MNCs, we have seen many repeats of this story in MNCs of other nationalities, including MNCs from developed countries with long histories of operating outside their home countries. From our own experiences and the studies we have read, we have concluded that a lot of companies from the rich countries look a lot more like Japanese companies than we would care to admit. They globalize their activities, but not their leadership. In the end, they slide backward and rarely recover."

Sounded a lot like AFG.

"The relevance of the lessons for companies based in developing countries such as Brazil, Russia, India or China, may be even more salient. According to what we have read, the experts don't believe that any national, cultural or economic factors make companies immune to the *Failure to Globally Launch* syndrome."

That somewhat soothed my wounded executive pride.

"The second major lesson is in the importance of building global leadership bench strength well *before* it is needed. Companies as diverse as Shell, PepsiCo, Nestlé, and IBM learned that developing global leaders was a necessary pre-cursor to a movement into the borderless global stage of development. This is similar to the lesson great players in team sports learn early in their training: If you want to make a long pass to an open teammate, you have to lead the teammate, and pass the ball not to where the teammate *is* but to where the teammate is *going to be*. A fundamental reason that successful global companies are largely passport blind with leadership talent is that they look down the line at what their leadership needs will *be* in the future—not what they are at the moment. They recognize that it takes time to build global leaders. They understand that if you wait until you need them, it's too late.

"I stress this point because, even though over the past decade China has added a net of 35 firms to the *Fortune Global 500* list, and Russia has added seven firms and India six, we see signs that many of these firms are more similar to the Japanese companies than to IBM, Shell, Nestlé or PepsiCo. Home country nationals still dominate their top ranks. They are lagging and not leading in building global leadership bench strength.

"Don't fool yourself into believing this is only a Japanese or Chinese problem," he cautioned. "Many firms in developed countries such as Germany, France and the U.S., particularly those new to the *Global 500* list in the last several years, also run the risk of falling off the list they fought so hard to join. Why? Because they too haven't moved fast enough at globalizing their bench strength."

Bench strength. Okay, what next?

Hans glanced at me. "Any more questions?"

"No, thank you. Go on, please."

"OK. Third, and perhaps most important, the failure of yesterday's Japanese success stories illustrates the fundamental axiom we have seen across companies that fail to globally launch, as well as companies that succeed. It is human nature to rely on people you know and trust. You generally know and trust people around you more than you trust people who are not."

He paused, looking directly at me. "This tendency is so strong that successful companies such as IBM and PepsiCo don't try to fight it. It is an unwinnable war. Instead, successful global companies fight the battle that *precedes* the war. They recognize that, left to their natural course, people get to know and trust those around them. Every corporate headquarters in the world is located in a particular country. If left unaltered, people at headquarters get to fully know and trust only the people from the country in which the headquarters is located. This means that they leave out entire swaths of talented people in the global company—some of whom have the potential to contribute far more than they are ever allowed. Companies around the world are short-changing themselves unless they take deliberate countermeasures to offset the natural pattern."

He turned to Anjanette. "For ideas about overcoming these problems, I'll turn the presentation over to Mademoiselle Bernard." Hans returned to his seat.

CHAPTER

27

NURTURING GLOBAL LEADERS

"THANK YOU, HANS." ANJANETTE ROSE AND WALKED TO THE FRONT OF THE room. "After comparing the differences between companies that succeed with their global launches and those that 'fall back to Earth,' we have developed four key tactics that we are using in our company today." Anjanette then put up a PowerPoint slide summarizing these tactics (see Figure 27-1).

Jacques interrupted. "David, I hope you find these suggestions useful. In fact, what Anjanette is going to tell you may well be the most important lessons you can take away from our discussion."

Anjanette continued, "The first tactic we found useful is what we call 'inpatriation.' There is no changing the fact that power will always reside at a company's global headquarters. Successful companies understand that if you want powerful people to know and trust those who are not citizens of the headquarters country, you must introduce a good number of foreigners into the mix. Phone, fax, video-conference, and email are not, and will likely never be, enough to establish the requisite knowledge and trust between head office people and non-citizens. Rubbing shoulders works far better."

I jotted "inpatriation" down. I liked the term.

"Here is an example: Nestlé's headquarters, which is less than an

Figure 27-1

4 Key Tactics in Nurturing Global Leaders

1. **Inpatriation**
   - Move foreigners to HQ to add variety, change the mix, prepare next generation of leaders

2. **Early Expatriation**
   - Send high-potential, young talent out into the world early

3. **Global Leadership Development**
   - Provides structure and helps people make sense of the world

4. **Use of Powerful Global Symbols**
   - Publicize role models & recognize global leadership successes

hour's drive from here, feels more like the United Nations than a Swiss company. Why? Because Nestlé uses management talent from around the world at its head office. They hold positions from the most junior to the most senior levels in the company. This ensures that key decision makers get to know the best people, regardless of where they were born or raised. It also helps to build talent that can be strategically used anywhere in the world where Nestlé operates."

No wonder Nestlé was kicking Snack Food butt. I raised my hand with a question. "What if the best and the brightest don't want to pull up stakes and move to headquarters? As nice as Switzerland is, it is certainly not for everyone. My wife felt this way about Lyon."

Jacques laughed. "How do you think we Europeans feel? Do you think we love St. Louis or Cleveland? You *have* to be kidding."

Anjanette added, "All true, but very few companies have headquarters in countries and cities that people refuse to go to. Maybe Vevey is nicer than St. Louis; maybe you prefer the freedom in the U.S. to the structure in Switzerland. In the end, it probably doesn't matter too much. If you work for Nestlé, you know that even if Vevey is not your most preferred destination in the world, it is where HQ is, and if you want a seat at the C-suite table someday, you have to know the people who sit at the table today. Same for AFG and St. Louis."

She continued, "Our second countermeasure is 'early expatriation.' If left unaided, it would be easy for the leaders of companies such as BASF, Carrefour, and Caterpillar, which have their headquarters in countries with large domestic markets, to overlook the talent, customers, and opportunities outside their home countries. This is why these companies and others send high-potential young talent out into the world early. These companies can afford this because the young talent is often sent with less than the luxurious packages than would be common for mid-career and higher expatriates. Those who accept the assignments believe that in exchange for less generous packages today, they will enjoy better career opportunities tomorrow."

"Hmm." I stroked my chin. If it worked for these companies, why not Snack Foods?

Anjanette continued, "Colgate-Palmolive has gone so far as to make some form of international experience a hiring requirement for young employees coming into its marketing function. Ernst & Young uses expatriation not only as a way to build judgment and leadership skills, but also as a retention tool for its young managers. These companies and others make sure they get their high-potential younger employees rubbing shoulders with people from various nationalities early in their careers."

I glanced at Jacques. "That's one thing I did right. Sarah and I did move to Lyon very early in my own career. It wasn't always fun, but it had a huge impact on me and my career."

Jacques nodded.

Anjanette went on, "The third countermeasure is organizing formal *global leadership development* training and development programs. The content of these development programs not only features global business and leadership training, but also includes people with globally diverse backgrounds as participants. We know that Shell, for example, runs its Group Business Leadership Program for high-potential middle managers, which involves participants from every region of the world and includes content designed to build global business and cross-cultural competencies. This is done intentionally as a way of exposing executive participants to diverse ideas and cultures."

I immediately thought of Ron's cost-cutting frame of mind. "Sounds expensive."

Hans said, "More expensive than the costs of losing your best people? After all, how much does it cost to lose, replace, and retrain a new manager?"

Anjanette added, "In many cases, global leadership development programs include multiple modules that bring the participants together more than once, engaging in learning projects and activities that keep them connected even when they are back home and physically separated. Other companies, like Nestlé, require that all managers participate in the 'Program for Executive Development' as a pre-requisite for advancement to the most senior ranks of the company. This program, run by a major business school in Switzerland, includes participants from a wide variety of companies and geographies and is valued because of its exposure to best practices and approaches *outside* the world of Nestlé."

I wondered if I could ever persuade Ron and the board to send our execs to an executive program outside the world of AFG.

"Finally, countermeasure four centers on the use of powerful symbols." Anjanette looked at me to be sure I was following. "Executives at successful global companies understand the value of symbols to signal what is important and what is not. Symbols are an efficient and effective way of focusing attention and helping people reassess priorities.

"One of the most useful symbols in companies," she explained, "involves the management of high-potential talent. Companies that get globalization right use high-profile promotions and the placement of non-home-country national employees in senior positions as a way of signaling that global talent is valued, recognized, and that a culture biased in favor of home-country employees is coming to an end. These companies also selectively recruit outsiders to signal that they value best practices, regardless of location."

Anjanette went on to explain that employees pay close attention to the people who serve in senior positions, not just because of their direct influence, but also because they symbolize the importance the company places on foreigners.

"HSBC has identified and set apart a group it calls International Managers or IMs, not only because of their technical skills, but also to communicate to local employees that global issues are important. HSBC employs about 350 IMs from every corner of the world—from both developed and developing countries."

She said that once people join the International Management track, the bank essentially controls their career path. They may stay two or three years in one location and then move to a new country. HSBC will typically employ three IMs in each country: the country CEO, the CFO, and someone else (often the head of audit or treasury). Every year, only a small number of people are privileged to move into the ranks of IM from within the bank. The IMs receive special benefits and recognition. However, because they come from everywhere and anywhere in the world, they are a powerful reminder to the rank and file that global issues matter and that you don't have to come from the U.K. or Hong Kong to make it into the top ranks of the company.

"David," Anjanette said, "I hope these four countermeasures make sense to you. They don't just happen without strong leadership. They are deliberate and anything but an accident."

"I'm beginning to understand the nature of our challenges and was starting to formulate action plans in my mind." I still couldn't quite get my head around the loyalty issue. So I asked her what I thought was a vital follow-up question. "Okay, Anjanette, let's assume that you are right. Let's assume that all these steps help prepare a new generation of what we can call global leaders. It still doesn't generate the kind of leaders who are loyal to the company. Skills and loyalty are quite different. Without loyalty, skills can be quite dangerous. In fact, if you do all the things you mentioned and the person leaves the company anyway, you've just financed the development of a global leader for your competitor. You might just as well have written them a check for $500,000 and not bothered with all the effort."

Anjanette didn't miss a beat. "It is important that you don't take this personally. I've now heard you say a few times that you were not able to find international managers who were as loyal to Snack Foods as were most Americans."

"Yes," I said, waiting for the next slap on my knuckles.

"What does loyalty mean to you?" she asked.

I answered quickly. "It's understanding that sometimes you have to put your own interests aside for the good of the entity to which you are loyal."

"This sounds straightforward," Anjanette replied. "After our discussion today, can you consider some of these so-called rebel leaders believed they had Snack Food's best interest in mind? Perhaps they were trying to adapt *The Snack Foods Way* to *The Way* of their country to help the business succeed in their market?"

I acknowledged the possibility with a shrug and a half smile.

"Through the countermeasures I have given you, the objective is to develop leaders who can move from focusing on solely the home market to the difficult task of not only paying attention to many different markets, but also embracing a broader perspective of loyalty. Beyond international business skills, the ideal global manager should be able to connect with people from incredibly diverse backgrounds and cultural orientations. They should make decisions without prejudice or giving the appearance of bias.

"Needless to say, this doesn't happen overnight," Anjanette emphasized. "But if your management realizes the tremendous value of this type of leader and then prioritizes the cultivation of these skills, you will create a much more effective organization."

CHAPTER

28

JOINT VENTURES AND MERGERS AND ACQUISITIONS

I WAS IMPRESSED BY HANS AND ANJANETTE'S PRESENTATIONS, BUT NOW I had at least two questions for every answer they offered.

Sensing this, Jacques asked, "Any more questions, David?"

"A few." I glanced at my notes and tried to organize my thoughts. "I think my questions can be summarized under two categories. First, I'm not convinced that incorporating more foreign nationals into senior management ranks is the answer to all of our problems, and second, grooming young talent is a process that takes years. Snack Foods needs to act *now* to turn things around. Unfortunately, the changes we need should have happened a long time ago."

As Hans and Anjanette were about to respond, Jacques leaned forward. "Of course, we are not suggesting that these countermeasures are a one-stop solution for all that ails you. We are pointing out that *all* companies face big challenges on the path to globalization, and those that *fail* follow similar patterns. The failures stem from an inability to globalize the leadership pipeline. This leads to an inability to globalize the people in the top ranks, both current and future leaders. Without top-level leaders who fully *get* globalization, multinational companies, like yours, are seriously disadvantaged. They are disadvantaged because they lack the experience, judgment, and expertise to manage a complex configuration of enterprises that globally integrate, locally differentiate, and otherwise blend the correct sets of activities for the business. It takes a while, but gradually their ambitions for global greatness unravel, with negative consequences."

"But—" I wanted a more concrete solution.

"Hear me out," Jacques said. "The paradox of globalization is that early successes can set the organization up for failure later, when the time comes to jump the final hurdle of globalizing leaders. People who are great performers within teams that think and act alike are rarely successful when the environment changes and they have to work with new colleagues, customers, suppliers and regulators who think differently. Developing and motivating talented people of *all* cultures and elevating them to meaningful roles in the company are essential if even modest global strategies are to succeed."

"Okay. I got it. We failed. Now what do we do?"

Hans took over. "In the short term, we think there are two main options that, when used judiciously, can dovetail with the internal counter-measures Anjanette discussed earlier. You might be surprised by these options: they are international joint ventures and mergers and acquisitions."

International Joint Ventures

Hans explained joint ventures have a number of benefits when it comes to promoting more diversity among the management ranks. First, because joint ventures are not takeovers, there is far less risk of destroying the prevailing culture of each partner's company. In turn, this will increase the likelihood that talent from each side will stay in place and not run for the exits.

Second, through joint ventures, in-house talent can be tested for leadership quality, as well as cultural skills. In some circumstances, international joint ventures or JVs also represent a source for future recruits. The American managers who are seconded to an international JV will come under intense pressure to adjust both their values and approaches to business. Hans explained, "Over time, the impact can be profound on JV leaders as well as their companies.

I started to grasp where Hans was coming from. "Because the pressure to adjust the business approaches will come about organically," I said, "and not because of orders issued from above, changes would probably meet with less resistance. Our American managers would more likely than not reach conclusions about diversity on their own. Senior management wouldn't need to use hard-sell tactics to obtain their buy-in."

Hans smiled and nodded. "Most of the American managers will see the need to adjust to conditions without having to be told. Plus, international joint ventures are useful as talent breeding grounds. You can send your employees to the JV for short assignments, helping them learn best practices and develop a broader perspective of other markets, cultures, management approaches, and more."

Hans pointed out that joint ventures also presented options for future acquisitions, without requiring large upfront commitments of time and resources. "The joint ventures themselves can be scaled up or down, depending on market conditions. In growth scenarios, JVs can be expanded. This translates into a diminishing reliance on American managers in the JV's overall value creation model. In difficult times, the JV can be wound up with limited risk to the parent company."

My mind raced. I couldn't believe that I hadn't more seriously considered this option before.

International M&As

"Mergers and acquisitions also offer a relatively quick approach to broadening the ranks of non-American management," Hans continued. "If you cannot build the people from within, or if there are strategic limits on your potential to benefit from joint ventures, the next best option is to *buy* a solution to your human capital problem."

I nodded. "In retrospect, this all seems so obvious."

"Many deep-pocketed companies worldwide have waited too long to do this," said Jacques. "Once you get off the sidelines, the question becomes, How do we best structure such deals? If you are concerned about broadening the ranks of management in the company *overall*, the deals must reflect that goal." Hans then put up a PowerPoint slide that provided some structure to his presentation (see Figure 28-1).

Figure 28-1:
Post-Acquisition Strategies

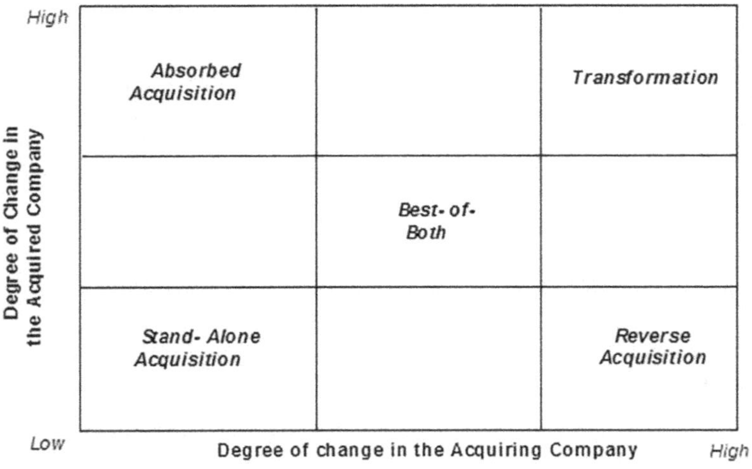

Hans added, "The three most common post-acquisition strategies include stand-alone acquisitions, absorbed acquisitions, and best-of-both mergers. Best-of-both mergers take what is good in both companies and then blend them. Both companies change and a new company is formed in the process. Best-of-both mergers have the added appeal of being relatively easy to sell, particularly to shareholders and top employees. After all, mergers are a lot less threatening than wholesale acquisitions. One approach, to globalization in general and globalizing your management specifically, would be to use best-of-both mergers as a fast track to getting there."

Hans shared the story of Nippon Sheet Glass and Pilkington of the United Kingdom as a good example of a best-of-both merger. Founded in 1918 as American Japan Sheet Glass, the company started by importing valuable glass-making technology from Libby Owens Ford Glass in the U.S. In 1931, the company officially changed its name to Nippon Sheet Glass (or NSG). After World War II, NSG grew in Japan and went on a buying binge, gobbling up Nippon Safety Glass, Nippon Glass Fiber, Micro Optics, and Nippon Muki Company.

Pilkington was one of NSG's major competitors. In 1986, it had purchased Libby Owens Ford, NSG's original supplier of technology. Worried about losing its technological edge, NSG purchased 20 percent of Pilkington in 2001. Five years later, it purchased the remaining 80 percent. The purchase effectively doubled NSG's size, giving it manufacturing operations in twenty-nine countries and sales in 130. The post-acquisition strategy was clearly best of both. By working together, NSG and Pilkington could improve production efficiencies, better underwrite technology investments, and improve penetration of emerging markets. As a sign of the seriousness of their commitment to a best of both approach, the NSG Group appointed Stuart Chambers (the former CEO of Pilkington) as its president. This was the first non-Japanese president that NSG employees had ever seen. Of the 35 senior executives of the company, seventeen were now non-Japanese nationals.

There was a drawback. "Unfortunately," Hans shrugged, "best-of-both mergers are difficult to successfully achieve even in the best of times. They promise diversity, market access, and an immediate bump in sales and profits, but they are tricky to implement. I would advise caution in taking this approach because these mergers are fraught with difficulty, even within the same national culture, let alone cross-culturally. For example, who makes decisions when you have to decide best-of-both? What happens to customers during the years it takes to integrate cultures? What happens to employee morale and trust if building the new organization drags on and on? They can be an expensive shortcut to globalizing your leadership."

Hans explained that NSG was smart to diversify the ranks of its top executives, but getting seventeen non-Japanese to work with eighteen Japanese peers was a huge challenge that didn't quickly resolve itself. Unless the leadership team is committed to making it work and until they receive a lot of cross-cultural and communications training, taking a best-of-both approach to mergers and acquisitions can be a formula for customer alienation and talent flight.

Which was *not* what I needed at this point. "What do you suggest then?"

Hans searched for additional material he wanted to show me. "I would suggest, if you are interested in broadening and *retaining* international talent, you consider the stand-alone acquisition option as a first choice. Companies pursuing stand-alone acquisitions get the best effects if they pursue these kinds of acquisitions in non-competing but related industries. They could be established as options on future uncertainties, scaling them up or down depending on opportunities. Because the parent company would have little or no experience in the new industry, its ability to add value through tinkering would be severely limited, reducing the temptation to absorb and smother the new venture. By leaving the acquisition alone, the existing management would be less likely to leave and more open to using the venture to incubate new ideas and new leaders. Because acquisitions usually command a premium price, a stand-alone venture becomes an expensive option. It would make the most sense if the acquisition met the dual imperatives of corporate diversification and leadership diversification, and if you can get a *deal.* "

CHAPTER

29

BURSTING BUBBLES AND BUILDING HOUSES

AT THIS POINT, ANJANETTE JUMPED BACK INTO THE DISCUSSION. "WHILE Hans likes to get into the big strategy topics like M&As, there are other less intrusive things you can do. First, Snack Foods has got to find ways to break down language barriers. Although your French is pretty good, I will bet that most of your American colleagues are not fluent in languages other than English."

I laughed. "I wouldn't take that bet."

"In my experience, the language abilities of top managers at American firms are mixed at best. Fluency means different things to different people, but assessments of foreign language skills are often inflated at American companies. I have seen this during meetings with American executives who are supposedly fluent in French or German, but are barely able to make themselves understood when ordering at a restaurant or asking directions to the nearest water closet."

"It's no secret that Americans have a reputation for weak language skills," I admitted. "We are actually pretty pathetic at it."

"But what is surprising," Anjanette continued, "is that even Americans who have graduated from good foreign language programs, and who are initially fluent in other languages, often see their skills degrade *after* coming home, despite considerable time overseas."

"You're right. I've had to work to keep my French up."

Anjanette nodded. "In my opinion, this is the result of companies insulating the employees from native people and cultures. When they live abroad, too many American business people communicate through translators and live and work in self-contained expatriate bubbles. They are not encouraged to immerse themselves in the language, culture, and business approaches of the host countries. They behave like holiday travelers who need not bother to adapt to the local environments."

"That's very true." All those years in France, and Sarah still struggled. In contrast, our daughters were taught by native speakers at the international school they attended and became very fluent.

"Now, my second point," Anjanette continued, "if you want to build a house, you first have to be clear on what you want the house to look like. Do you want it to be an Asian style, Swiss Chalet, Tudor, or an American Cape Cod? What functions do you want it to serve? Do you want to entertain many guests at the house, or is it only for the family? Similarly, if you want to build more global leaders, you must spend time defining what a *good global leader* looks like. And the last people you want to involved in building these new leaders are the existing executives. Their skills got them where they are today. They are masters of the old system—"

"*The Snack Foods Way*," I interrupted.

"Exactly," said Anjanette with Jacques nodding in agreement. "Although these existing executives may have some interesting ideas on what it will take to succeed in the future, the reality is that they will be retired for a long time before the skills of the next generation of leaders will become truly valued. No, it is better to look at the leadership needs and competencies required in the future to define what *good global leaders* look like."

Jacques sat back in his chair and folded his arms. "Tell him what we are implementing here."

"The review and definition process will involve our human resources staff, as well as thought leaders in the broader HR community. We will also include discussions with our strategic thinkers to better understand the direction of the company, the timing of key moves, and the competencies needed."

"You should do the same," Jacques suggested.

Anjanette broadened her discussion. "Every company organizes its people or human resource management systems differently, but I usually think of six major functions as critical." She explained that these functions are (1) recruitment, (2) engagement and retention, (3) identifying and developing high-potential employees, (4) performance management, (5) succession planning and management, and (6) training and development. She put up a PowerPoint slide reflecting these key functions (see Figure 29-1).

Figure 29-1
6 Key Functions of Human Resource Management

1. **Recruitment**
   - Ensuring the "right" people are on board
2. **Engagement and retention**
   - Ensuring that your people are focused on their jobs & happy with the company
3. **Identifying and developing high-potential employees**
   - Ensuring that your best people have been identified and given significant development opportunities
4. **Performance management**
   - Holding people accountable and providing them with differential rewards
5. **Succession planning and management**
   - Mapping the next generation of leaders, planning for departures and replacements of key leaders
6. **Training and development**
   - Providing meaningful development experiences, including on-the-job learning and formal training, for key employees

Anjanette explained that while some aspects of these functions will always have a local component, many firms lack a coherent model for globalizing their people management. Too often, corporate HR plays only a supporting role and exists merely to gather data and prepare reports. HR is viewed as tactical and operational but not as a strategic partner. This view must change if American companies are ever to effectively tackle the challenges of globalization.

I knew entire books had been written on how companies could globalize each of the six major HR management functions. In fact, I had read a few but had subsequently forgotten most of what I had learned. What Anjanette was saying reminded me that the key to globalizing HR was recognizing that not *all* supporting practices should indeed be globalized. Instead, consistent with embracing a truly borderless global model, the people solution needed a mixture of local, regional, and global approaches. A global competency model required some regional adaptations, as well as local performance assessments.

Ajnanette concluded, "The real challenge is to develop within the organization the capabilities and sophistication to complete this enormous task consistently and with the support and respect of the business lines." She then asked, "How is Snack Foods doing on defining the competencies of global leaders? How far has it gone to globalize HR?"

"Not far enough," was my response. An understatement if ever there was one.

Jacques leaned forward and gave me a sympathetic smile. "And there you have it. David, you must be exhausted. I know I am. Let's hit the slopes."

As Jacques and I skied the rest of the day, the germ of an idea grew into the beginnings of a plan in my mind. Though I wasn't yet able to verbalize the strategies that my brain was feverishly assessing at the semi-conscious level, I was confident that I could now find a way out of my predicament.

I knew what Harry Truman must have felt like in 1948. While experts predicted his imminent defeat in the upcoming election, Truman remained confident, though he didn't articulate in public the reasons for this confidence. Perhaps I was confident because, like Truman, my choices now were so stark and utterly clear. I would either go down in flames after proposing my solutions to the Snack Foods global expansion crisis, or my report would become one of my greatest triumphs. I would either rescue Snack Foods from the doldrums or face an early retirement.

I've read that a crisis can either make or break a leader. I was a living example. I had nothing to lose and everything to gain by proposing a bold new course of action. What's more, I was convinced that I was finally on the right path. My challenge would be persuading Ron Walker and the board this was not just the best way forward, but the *only* way forward.

If only I had some new ideas on how to rescue my marriage.

CHAPTER

30

ACTION PLAN

THE DAY AFTER I MET WITH JACQUES AND HIS TEAM IN VERBIER, I RETURNED to an empty house in St. Louis. Still, I felt energized and rejuvenated. I was *so* energized that it was impossible for me to sleep or sit still.

The next morning I decided I would work from home. I phoned my assistant and asked her to cancel or reschedule all of my appointments, hold all of my calls, and tell anyone who asked that I was too ill to come to the office. I then headed to the nearest Radio Shack where I purchased a digital voice recorder. During the next three days, I paced the house and took long walks maniacally recording every idea that spilled from my feverish brain. In the evenings, I tried watching television, but the volume remained muted as I jotted down one thought after another on the nearest magazine cover, napkin, envelope, even a coaster. I fell asleep on the sofa, woke up, and went back to work.

I tacked my printouts and handwritten notes to a corkboard in my home office, creating a vast collage that looked like something from the movie *A Beautiful Mind*. I entered the data into a Word document to better arrange my ideas.

The first fruit of my mental renaissance was a trip to my local travel agency where I arranged a flight to Tahiti for two people. First class. Then I called my wife.

"How is Jacques?" She sounded down.

"Jacques is amazing." I lowered my voice. "What I want to know is how are you?"

"Fine." She sounded on the verge of tears.

"I have a proposal."

"Nothing has changed."

"Okay, but I was just wondering. Would you be interested in joining me for a series of self-guided marriage counseling sessions in the South Pacific?" It came out kind of corny, but I meant every word.

She sensed how sincere I was. "Dave." She said it slowly and her voice trailed off.

I had a chance.

"How about we talk things through at the St. Regis in Bora Bora?"

"Bora Bora." Her voice took on a dreamy tone.

"I do listen to you sometimes."

"I don't want to give up, but I'm not sure your trip to Switzerland and a couple of days hanging out with Jacques will have magically transformed you."

"Of course not. Change comes slowly and is not easy, but you can have moments when you suddenly see the light, can't you?" I purposely waited. I had to wait longer than I thought I would.

"Yes, of course you can suddenly see the light, but that doesn't mean you instantly change your behavior."

"You're right, but without seeing the light, you have no chance, right?" This time I didn't wait for an answer. "Look I'm not promising that I will transform overnight, but I am saying the need to change has never been more clear in my life." I took a deep breath and lowered my tone of voice. "My desire to change has never been stronger. Just say you will seriously consider it."

"Okay."

With my marriage resuscitation plan on track, I could turn my full concentration to saving my job—and Snack Foods. I decided to take another week at home to create an action plan. Only then would I go back to the office to begin adding meat to the bones.

I had listened intently to Jacques and his team's presentation, excited by their insights into globalization and the reasons for failure of many companies. I determined that a fully American approach was no longer appropriate for Snack Foods. At the same time, the company should not aspire to a wholly foreign approach, either. We needed to globally integrate some activities and localize others, but most of all, we needed to globalize our leadership.

When Ron had first ordered me to present to the board, in my haste to generate the numbers I'd focused on the hardware and not the software. To fix the business and capitalize on the benefits of globalization, I had to address five separate challenges:

- Changing the organizational structure
- Fixing my team
- Building key capabilities
- Adapting the organization's culture
- Renewing myself

These would become my priorities and the pillars of my action plan.

CHAPTER
31

CHANGING THE ORGANIZATIONAL STRUCTURE

SNACK FOODS WAS SLOWLY FAILING IN THE MARKETPLACE; IT WAS FAILING operationally, and it was failing in employee morale.

I realized that many of these problems were rooted in our overly rigid structure. It was now clear to me that our top-down, U.S.-centric approach wasn't working. Our bottom-up approach had also been a failure, because it added costs and complexity without capitalizing on the advantages associated with global reach: global sourcing, global learning/technology, and global brands.

I decided that Snack Foods' traditional structure had to go. Globalization could not be *forced* on Snack Foods. But I could *lead* the company forward using a hybrid structure, one that was more flexible and responsive to the ever-changing realities of the marketplaces.

Snack Foods had been organized using an area structure that included Europe, North America (Canada/U.S.), Latin America, and Asia/Pacific. The structure worked well for most marketing activities, but did not work for other activities. Instead of trying to find the perfect structure, I opted to address Snack Foods' organizational challenges by focusing more on activities and systems, and less on the formal organization chart.

What we needed was fluid organizational systems.

Using a fluid systems approach, the organizational structure would *never* be static. I wouldn't even try to organize a neat solution that could easily be mapped or classified. Activities like purchasing, HR, finance, and IT would clearly benefit from central control out of St. Louis. Although they would be centralized, these activities would necessarily require local input and staff. Other activities, namely marketing, product development, and manufacturing, would be turned over to the Areas to manage. Even here, I expected that area managers would defer all kinds of decisions to even more local leaders. For example, activities such as sales and sales promotion would *mostly* be controlled at the country level. In some cases, promotion would differ even at the level of sales districts within countries.

In Europe, where the company had now been operating for over two decades, the quality of local leaders was much stronger than in Latin America or parts of Asia. In Europe, deferring decisions to local managers made more sense than in a country like Paraguay, where Snack Foods had a small and immature staff. A fluid organization would reflect the reality that each Area looked different. It would also reflect the reality that, as the organization matured, the structure could evolve. It had to evolve.

Although the model was clear in my mind, I was sure that others would neither understand it nor embrace it because it lacked traditional clarity. To overcome this obstacle, I would move forward with a combination of simple communications combined with a few tangible, structural tweaks.

The communications focused on clear messages based on rock-solid certainty: going forward, we would have global vice presidents of Finance, Purchasing, IT and HRM. Each would be based out of headquarters in St. Louis. The Areas would be fully responsible for everything else. It would be up to the Areas to sort out other roles and responsibilities down to the country level.

Overlaid on this clarity were three additional structural tweaks.

First, IT would be expanded to include knowledge management. This would involve capturing best practices (both inside and outside the business) and disseminating that knowledge globally within Snack Foods. It would also require the global organization to put appropriate technologies in place to effectively compete.

Second, Area Boards would be created, composed of the functional heads controlled by the Areas *plus* representatives from global Finance, HRM, IT/Knowledge, and Purchasing from St Louis.

I figured the added complexity of Area decision-making might overwhelm Area presidents. They would benefit greatly from the additional input of a formal board. Therefore, the final tweak would be the creation of a new Global Snack Foods Board that comprised Area presidents and St. Louis-based functional VPs. The Areas would be required to convene *their* Boards monthly; I would convene the Global Snack Foods Board every two months.

While the new organization wouldn't solve every problem, no structure would. The new structure was a great start and no doubt one that would please the people in the field—put smiles on their faces.

CHAPTER

32

FIXING MY TEAM

As the organizational structure changed, my team would have to change along with it. More than ever, members of my senior team would need to "walk the talk."

For the moment, I had seven direct reports—all of them Americans based at HQ in St. Louis. With the upgrade to a Global Snack Foods Board, I'd need to expand the number of direct reports to at least eight people (four from the Areas, plus Finance, HRM, IT/Knowledge, and Purchasing). I would achieve this by promoting the head of IT, who had previously reported to Finance, to Global VP of IT/Knowledge. He would now report directly to me.

But I didn't stop there.

I had recently conducted annual reviews for my seven current reports. Four scored outstanding, one was adequate, and two rated not meeting expectations. The last category included Peter Misinchuk, scheduled to retire in twelve months, and Bob McCain, the 52-year-old head of global marketing. I now decided that I would terminate McCain, which was justified on the merits alone but over which I'd procrastinated. If I acted now, the termination would (a) shift the locus of control for marketing from the center to the Areas; (b) signal to the organization that I would not tolerate poor performance; and (c) allow me to immediately bring in new talent from outside the company.

Before I terminated McCain, I called Hans Schroder, the former CEO of Snack Foods Germany. He'd greatly impressed me when I met with him and Anjanette at Jacques's company. I hated to pay back Jacques's good friendship and timely aid by poaching a senior executive, but Hans had the talent I needed now.

I offered Hans the Senior VP of Market Strategy slot (a new position) at a 40 percent pay increase over what he was making working for Jacques. Hans would be charged with coordinating global marketing efforts and helping me determine long-term strategy for the business, including joint ventures and acquisitions.

Hans would have two offices: a primary office in Europe, and a secondary office at HQ in St. Louis. I expected that about 70 percent of Hans' time would be spent in Europe, and the remainder either traveling or in St. Louis.

When I alerted Jacques about my plans to poach Hans, he was ready to accommodate me, believing the move would not only help me, but also strengthen the ties between his business and Snack Foods. "I saw this coming," he said. "Don't worry, you will have plenty of time to make up for this later."

I am not sure what he meant by this, and I must admit I had twinges of guilt, but I also think Jacques viewed Hans as someone who had contributed hugely to his organization's strategy, which was now mostly set. He came in and did a great job for Jacques's company, but now he could actually be more valuable to Jacques if he worked for me. I was relieved that Jacques seemed to see it this way as well! In fact, a big part of me suspected Jacques had orchestrated the entire thing when he invited Hans to his chalet in Verbier.

After Hans accepted the position, which would start in 30 days, I terminated McCain.

In addition to replacing one member of my senior team, I planned to announce a new policy at our next full management meeting of our top 64 executives. In order to join the newly formed Global Snack Foods Board in the future, senior leaders would have to be fluent in at least two languages. Those already on the board got a pass. This would help ensure that the members of the senior team would support the new policy.

I also met with Peter Misinchuk to explore early retirement options, and he agreed to a six-month buy-down of his contract. I informed my senior team that Peter would be leaving in six months and requested that they provide suggestions for his replacement. I made it clear that only non-Americans or Americans with serious international experience would be considered as his replacement.

CHAPTER
33

ADAPTING THE CULTURE

THERE WAS MUCH TO LOVE ABOUT THE EXISTING SNACK FOODS CULTURE. The old *Way* had served the business well, so I didn't want to toss it out. What I wanted was to leverage the good aspects of our culture while adding new components. I wanted to create a *New Global Way* that would require a commitment to:

- Say what you mean, and mean what you say. This component would remain unchanged. Yes, I realized that it was U.S.-centric. And yes, I knew people in countries such as Japan might be uncomfortable with this aspect of *The Way*. But given the cultural diversity of Snack Foods and the potential for miscommunication, I believed this aspect of the culture was critical to our future success.
- Another unchanged component was the emphasis on competing to win. In fact, I wanted to *strengthen* this element, moving it toward the top of the priority list.

New components of *The New Global Way* would include:
- Excellence in practices, regardless of where ideas came from.
- A commitment to customers in *attitude*, not just in skills. Just be-

cause people are skilled at solving customer problems doesn't mean they actually *like* the customers or want to champion them. The new focus on customer centricity would be about blending skills *and* attitude.

- Speed—in both decision-making and execution. We had clearly become complacent and slow. This had to change and it had to start at the core level of our values.
- Snack Foods first! This would be a key to achieving global cooperation.

I realized that no quick fixes were possible in adapting *The Way*. The key to changing the culture was getting members of the Area and global Snack Foods boards to walk the walk. For this reason, The New Global Way had to become a central theme in every aspect of the working lives of our senior leaders. On this dimension, there was much more that could and should be done.

CHAPTER

34

CAPABILITIES

I WANTED THE LEADERS OF THE NEW SNACK FOODS TO BE THOSE WHO thrived in fluid organizations and who relished getting things done correctly, rather than those who craved internal status. They would be people who could embrace ambiguity and work effectively in complex teams. They would be people who could develop and exploit global relationships, and find ways to become relevant beyond their set roles.

The stark reality was that the best people in the Snack Foods world included many who were not Americans, and these folks had been leaving the company in droves. I knew that without the best talent, Snack Foods would languish.

I'd long sensed Snack Foods needed a more sophisticated approach to leadership. Only now did I fully appreciate what that approach would require and how many years it would take to achieve. So as part of my preparation for the presentation to Ron Walker and the board of directors, I created a new leadership competency model for Snack Foods. With some help from HR, it didn't take long to do; I'd been thinking about it for some time. I determined that a great Snack Foods leader had to possess five core competencies:

- Customer centricity
- Inspirational direct personal leadership
- Strategic acumen
- Organizational savvy
- Business savvy

The wording in this list was not very different from that in our old model. It was the *meaning* of the words that I determined would change.

What would each competency look like? How would it *feel*? How would the competency model play out in managing people's performance? These were questions that the new global Snack Foods board would need to answer.

In order to fully capture their attention, I determined that starting this year, Global Snack Foods board members and Area board members would be assessed according to (a) their business results and (b) their competencies (based on the five-point model). By assessing them in year one, defining the competency components would become a top priority for my senior leaders. I also decided board members receiving *unsatisfactory* scores on any dimension would be given one year to improve to *satisfactory* or they'd be terminated. In year two, business performance and competency assessments would be extended down to the next 120 leaders in the organization. In year three, over 500 Snack Foods leaders would be assessed with the competency model.

In addition to putting pressure on the global and area board members, I turned to my vice president of human resources management, Phil Nesbit, for assistance in rounding out the competency development process. Specifically, I asked him to:

- **Create a *New Way* Leadership Academy**. This would be based, not in St. Louis, but near Frankfurt, Germany to signal the importance of international sales and non-U.S. employees to the success of Snack Foods. I determined that every year, middle-to-senior managers at Snack Foods would spend a minimum of two weeks at the Academy. A mixture of Global and Area Board members and outside professors would teach classes and facilitate discussions. I also decided that every member of my Global Board would teach or facilitate at the Academy for at least ten half-days per year. Fully 25 percent of their bonus would be based on feedback scores received from participants.

- **Create a new category of international executives.** These would be mid-level managers, initially numbering twelve people, and growing to about 50 people within three years. These managers would be rotated every two years from one location to another, sometimes coming to the U.S. but mostly moving between other countries. They would bring much-needed technical skills to these countries and would also serve as ambassadors of *The New Global Way*. Eventually, they would help build an invaluable global management network.

- **Introduce a best practices forum under the direction of the VP of IT/Knowledge.** I determined that once a year, middle managers and above would be required to present to their boss's boss, in a one-day forum, a best practice of practical use to Snack Foods, either dreamed up or borrowed from a company outside the food industry. Each supervising boss would be given a budget to reward the best idea with a bonus equaling 100 percent of the employee's salary. Also once a year, the company would organize a global best practices forum, wherein the boss's boss and the winning employee would present *their* chosen best practice to the Global Snack Foods board. The board would then choose two best practices for implementation throughout at least one region of the world. If chosen, the boss's boss would also receive a bonus of 100 percent of current salary. The employee who had developed the best practice would receive another bonus of 100 percent of salary. Money always talks, and I was certain that this best practices forum would get people's full attention.

Finally, I asked our CFO together with Hans, our new VP of Market Strategy, and Phil Nesbit, VP of Human Resource Management, to work together to develop a review process for JVs and acquisitions. Central to the review would be an annual assessment of JV and acquisition options for each overseas affiliate. The criteria would be weighted equally by the strategic benefits of possible deals, immediate growth and profit opportunities, and talent benefits that would come by working closely with partner or acquired company.

CHAPTER
35

RENEWING MYSELF

I NOW UNDERSTOOD THAT I HADN'T GROWN ENOUGH AS A LEADER. AS MY world became more complex, I had compensated by trying to exert more control over the uncertainties, which I did by increasing my power as well as the power of head office, forcing a head-office mentality on everyone else. My come-to-Jesus moment with the AFG Board had shaken me to the core, and my rocky marriage had convinced me that success and happiness could not be guaranteed. I would have to change. I would have to reorganize my priorities and rearrange my approach to leadership. This was not going to be easy. Years of success and selective filtering of the facts had reinforced my bad habits.

Central to this was a decision to approach my job at Snack Foods from a fundamentally new perspective. Rather than manage the organization, I would lead it. This would mean focusing most of my efforts on the people. Whatever I wanted done would, from this time forward, be done through and by other people and not directly by me. I would delegate and hold people accountable. I would spend much more time coaching my people and clarifying my definition of what good looked like.

This approach would mean that I had to let go and surrender routine tasks and low-value activities. Most important, it meant surrendering my psychological need to have all the answers to all possible questions. Snack

Foods had become too large for me to manage and control by myself. Leadership meant ensuring the right people and the right systems were in place and the organization was strategically positioned for success.

Additional changes to my style would be required in areas I couldn't yet foresee. I also appreciated that without ongoing coaching, I risked sliding back into old behaviors. To ensure this didn't happen, I swallowed my pride and asked for a confidential meeting with Ron Walker prior to my presentation to the board.

I suggested the meeting take place over dinner, far away from the office. I needed a casual environment so I could share my thoughts. I booked a private table at Ron's favorite restaurant. During the meeting, I reviewed my plans to change the organizational structure, fix my team, build key capabilities, and adapt the Snack Foods culture.

As I spoke, Ron listened intently and nodded regularly. He interrupted only occasionally with clarifying questions.

At the end of my explanation, Ron said, "These are great ideas, David. You're to be commended. As you move this forward, I'm sure you'll clarify your thinking even further. I'd like to discuss this again before your presentation to the board." After a pause, he asked, "Anything else on your mind?"

"Ron, you've been a wonderful help to me. I wouldn't be here without your support. I know you're busy, so I don't want to drain too much time from you. But I could use some help. Could we identify a member of the AFG Board, perhaps one of the three who is a retired CEO, with whom I could meet regularly? I need some coaching."

A broad smile spread across Ron's face. "Yes, I think we can arrange that."

Later, Ron asked Paul Jefferson, former CEO of a Fortune 50 company and a board member of AFG, if he would meet with me to offer support and guidance. He gladly accepted the invitation. We met a week before my presentation to the board. I laid out my plans and asked for his feedback.

After a good discussion, I asked if he were amenable to regular get-togethers. "Just informal chats."

He readily agreed.

Over time, Paul and I became close friends. He not only helped guide me in preparing for board meetings, but also offered invaluable longer term coaching on my five priorities.

CHAPTER

36

MEETING WITH THE BOARD

THE THREE WEEKS RON HAD GIVEN ME TO PREPARE FOR THE BOARD MEETING went by in a flash. I decided to forego the normal PowerPoint slides and speak from the heart. Well, kind of. To help the heart, I prepared four note cards. The first card addressed how we got ourselves into our current problems, the second addressed structural and organizational solutions, the third card addressed the people issues, and the final card covered my personal takeaways. I kept each card simple, with a maximum of 5 bullets.

Ron had asked me to arrive at the boardroom for a 10:45 AM slot on the agenda and indicated that the board had allocated 30 minutes for my presentation. In those brief minutes, the board would measure me by how I presented as much or more as what I presented. His assistant called me late in the afternoon the day before my presentation and asked if I wanted to share any written material with the board in advance.

"No," I answered. This is what speaking from the heart meant.

On the morning of the board presentation, I awoke alone and exhausted. I'd spent the previous night in 30-minute installments of sleep, interrupted by cold sweat and heart palpations.

After shaving and showering, I put on my best navy blue banker's suit and nicest Hermes tie. I added a pair of silver AFG cufflinks, hoping that my company loyalty might somehow score a few psychological points. I went to the office and asked my secretary, Alice, to hold all calls. I walked to my office window and stared at the St. Louis skyline. As I did, my mind drifted back to the earlier board meeting, less than a month ago. The memories of embarrassment and humiliation flooded my mind and a feeling of overwhelming anxiety and near panic hit me. I could not go through that again.

As I stood looking out the window, I felt the tingle of a bead of sweat form on my temple. Then I muttered to myself, "Why am I wasting my time stressing when I should be preparing what I will say?"

I drew my notes cards out of my breast pocket and reviewed them. My breathing slowed, and my spirits began to calm. For the next 30 minutes, I rehearsed my presentation.

At 10:30, Alice rapped lightly on my door. "It's time to head up to your meeting."

Unlike my last board meeting, this time I sat in the wood-lined lobby outside the boardroom feeling calm and relaxed. I had a good plan, and I would deliver it with confidence.

At 10:50, the door to the boardroom opened. Ron Walker extended his hand, smiled and said, "You're up." As I walked past him, he whispered, "I have them all primed. You'll do fine."

I entered the inner sanctum of AFG, the infamous board of directors' conference room. As I walked in, I paused to survey the room. I counted 11 directors, all over 60 years old. It was a full house. I was surprised they all showed up. Maybe they were expecting to have some fun. Nine of the directors were men; two were women. They sat around the large, polished mahogany table in swivel, black leather chairs. I noticed framed pictures of past CEOs going back a century or more on the boardroom walls. I wondered how many deaths by firing had occurred in this room over the years? Would I be another in a long line of casualties? Glancing down at the wool carpeting underfoot, I wondered if it was thick enough to soak up the blood that would soon be spilt?

None of the directors smiled. The room was eerily quiet.

As I walked to the empty seat at the head of the table, I was happy that each director had a nametag on the table in front of their seat. This had a calming effect on me. While I had met all of them on multiple occasions since becoming President of Snack Foods, I only had what I would describe as a close relationship with a handful of them.

After I sat down, Ron began to speak. "We are pleased that David could join us. As you may recall, his previous presentation raised a number of questions, and he is here to address those questions. David, take it away."

All eyes fixed on me.

I rose to my feet. "Thank you Ron. It's a pleasure to be back here with all of you." I wondered if they knew exactly how big a lie that was? I went on. "I appreciate and understand your concern expressed before about the state of our business. I share your concern. Fixing this business and setting it on the right course is my single priority.

"We are all proud of what we have accomplished and built in Snack Foods, but we can do better. We must do better. Before I describe my plan of action, let me take a few minutes to discuss how we got to where we are." I glanced down at my first card to refresh my memory. As I proceeded to review the key points, I looked to the directors for some reaction. Any reaction.

There was none. They sat, stone faced.

I reviewed the path that got us to our present point.

Still, no reaction from anyone.

I continued, "Now that we have reviewed some history, let me discuss with you my plan to move us forward."

Several of the directors leaned forward in their chairs. I finally seemed to have their attention.

"The first leg of my plan is a change in the organization structure." I explained the creation of a more fluid organization, of a global Snack Foods Board and Area Boards. I looked around the room and, while I had their attention, I could not read a single reaction. They remained stone faced. I paused for a question. Nothing.

Sensing that I was losing them, I quickly shifted to the second element of my plan: building capabilities. A few people shifted in their seats. But then, nothing. No questions. I turned to Ron and noticed him quietly touch his right index finger to his watch. He did it so no one but me would notice. I looked at the clock on the back wall and realized that I had 15 minutes left before the Board would pull the plug on my presentation and career. I swallowed hard and determined to go out with a fight.

I put down my cards and began to talk about my team. "The third leg of my plan is to fix my team. You know I have a great bunch of people to work with. I realize the people who get you to where you are today often are not the same people who you need to get you to where you need to go tomorrow. I have been thinking a lot about how to deal with this. Today, I am reporting the replacement of two of my direct reports. I am also reporting the creation of a new VP of Strategy, a position to be filled by Hans Schroder."

This elicited the first question from the Board. "Is this the same Hans Schroder who left the company a few years ago. Why would you want to bring him back?" A few other directors nodded in agreement.

"Excellent question. My answer may surprise you. He wants to come back because he believes in my vision for this business. We need him back because of how he can contribute to this vision."

The first director interjected, "Tell us more about this vision."

I explained that the future for Snack Foods was global. Not American. Not European. A business without borders. I talked about our need to fill the world with AFG snacks. I explained that the future lay outside the US, where 95% of the world's population resided. I confessed that my team and, in fact, I were too blinded by our own American-ness to fully see the potential in front of us.

"Are you suggesting that we walk away from what made us great?" a director asked.

"Not at all." I shook my head for emphasis. "We don't need to walk away from anything that is good. We should be proud of what we have done and who we are, but we need a different mix of people. We need a different kind of DNA. The markets we need to penetrate, the customers we need to win over, the distribution channels we need to dominate are quite different from here in the U.S. We need—I need—a team that has the depth of insight and understanding to help us win this battle. For this reason, I am introducing a new policy that in the future all senior members of the Global Snack Foods board be fluent in two or more languages. If you are already a member of the board, you get a pass."

I explained my desire to globalize by adding an increasing number of non-Americans to this group. "This is why bringing someone like Hans Schroder back is such a good idea. He knows us, but he brings something entirely new. We need this. I need this." I made this impassioned speech with a level of confidence that surprised even me.

I looked up at the clock. It was 11:20. I was five minutes over. I turned to Ron.

He wasn't pointing at his watch. Instead, the next question was directed to him.

One of the directors asked, "Ron, Dave has some good ideas here. How does this fit in with AFG's vision for the future?"

Another asked, "What can we do to bring some of these ideas to the other divisions?"

Ron did not have any answers, but as a smart CEO he let them slide off with, "Now you see why I was confident that Dave was the man to turn things around. He's not only got a great view of where to take Snack Foods and how to move it forward but has stimulated some needed discussions regarding the entire company. Since we're a bit over time, I'd like to pick up these additional questions either later today or even better to set aside some dedicated time at our next board meeting."

My dinner companion and new board mentor, Paul Jefferson, interrupted Ron. "Ron," he said, "I would be delighted if David could spare us a little more time now."

The other directors nodded their agreement.

A broad smile spread across my face. "Of course." I continued with a broader discussion of the need to grow our capabilities and revise our culture.

What ensued was a rich and deep discussion, not so much about Snack Foods, but of the need to change the other parts of the business and AFG overall.

At 12:45, Ron stood to close off our meeting. "Ladies and gentlemen, our lunch is now getting cold. David, would you like to join us? You have been doing a lot of talking, and I am sure you must be hungry."

Over lunch, almost all of the directors came by to thank me or pat me on the shoulder and whisper a few positive remarks. Ron saved his comments until later.

At 4:30pm, Ron dropped by my office. I was emotionally exhausted and playing around on the computer when he walked in.

"David, you didn't disappoint. I heard nothing but good comments from the board. I think you raised our vision. I can't say I personally feel ready for a global AFG, but it is clear after our discussions today that we have no choice. We need help." He clapped a hand on my back. "And we need you."

I wasn't sure what this meant or where this would head, but now that I knew I wasn't getting fired, my number one thought was Sarah not Ron.

CHAPTER

37

BORA BORA

I dropped by my mother-in-law's house at 5:30 p.m. that afternoon. Hearing someone at the door, and maybe even recognizing my voice, Sarah started down the stairs. It was a bit of a cliché but I figured a dozen red roses and a dinner reservation at her favorite restaurant would win her over—at least for one night. And it did.

During dinner, I gave her an envelope and asked her to open it.

"What's inside?" she wanted to know.

"Open it and you'll find out," I replied.

She lifted the flap. Reservations for two first class tickets to Papeete, Tahiti peaked out at her. She looked behind the tickets and found a brochure for the IntereContinental Le Moana Bora Bora. Probably the best resort on the island.

She put the envelope down and smiled.

That's all I needed.

Before we left for Tahiti, I told my staff that I wouldn't look at email, so the only way to reach me was to call, and if they did call, it had better be because civilization as we knew it was coming to an end. Within the week, Sarah and I were winging our way to a much-needed reconnection.

I couldn't remember the last time I wasn't fretting about the job while on vacation. It was difficult, but I was true to my word and didn't check my email once. Civilization as we knew it did not come to an end, so no one from the office called. It taught me a great lesson: much of the intrusion of my work life into my personal life was at my invitation. Over the years, work had not been breaking down or barging through the door as an unwelcome intruder but was stepping through a door I left wide open and for which I had put a welcome mat.

The same was true for travel. Much of my travel in the past was designed to feed my unconscious need for information, control, and status. In a global business, I would have to travel. I needed a first hand feel for things and my people needed a first hand feel for me, but did that really require 200 days away from home a year? I committed to Sarah (and to myself) that I would limit my travel to half that amount or less. When I wasn't traveling, I promised to be home at least four nights a week before 7 p.m. Sarah was shocked but pleased.

Because this wasn't the first time that I had made commitments to change but had soon reneged, I knew that Sarah needed more than just promises to trust that this time would be different. As a consequence, I talked to her about how I had come to recognize that much of what drove me to travel, work late, be preoccupied with work even when at home or vacation was my own needs and not what the job needed from me. I saw that now. I recognized that it was actually holding back people around me at work and, most importantly, I recognized the price that she, the girls, and even I paid at home.

I wasn't sure what to expect at the end of this long but sincere disclosure, confession, and apology. I was prepared for Sarah to have a bit of an I'll-believe-it-when-I-see-it attitude.

Instead she smiled and then crystalized all that I had determined to change about work in one simple sentence. "So finally you are going to lead rather than run the business."

After we got home, I even agreed to a couple sessions with a marriage counselor. Sarah and I had never really fallen out of love, only gotten off track from appreciating each other and putting the other's needs ahead of busy schedules—or rather I had gotten off track, but now I was determined not to let that happen again.

CHAPTER

38

UNDERSTANDING THE GLOBAL WAY

THE STORY OF DAVE AND AFG IS AN ALL TOO COMMON ONE; A STORY BUILT ON the underlying phenomenon that what makes you successful at one stage of development often is *not* what is needed for success at the next stage. This is true for both the organization and for its leaders.

The development and preparation of the people must precede the development of the organization, or the organization will be unable to pull free of the gravitational pull of its past success. Just like a spacecraft breaking free of earth's gravitational pull, it is essential for companies to anticipate and fire the booster rockets that develop the people *before* they feel a deceleration of the organizational spacecraft. If astronauts wait until the spacecraft begins to slow down, the force needed to help it break free of the gravitational pull will be exponentially greater. At some point, they simply can't muster the power needed to avoid crashing back to earth. The same is true for companies. Despite a clear trajectory forward, without anticipating leadership needs, companies will fail to reach their global potential. What were once highflyers crash back to earth. You need only look at the 65 percent disappearance of Japanese firms from the *Fortune Global 500* list, the list they dominated fifteen years ago, to get a real-life illustration of how dramatically this can happen.

The Company's Global Way

Companies approach globalization with various tools and strategies at their disposal. Some companies are sophisticated in their preparations and complex in their approaches; others pursue simpler, bare-bones paths. Regardless of the approach, companies fundamentally have only two basic globalization tools at their disposal. First, they can sell their goods or services overseas by exporting or trading them. (Under the category of trade, international business theorists would include the flow of knowledge and expertise as well as products.) Second, companies can sell their goods or services overseas by investing in foreign countries and producing locally. Investments, or more properly Foreign Direct Investment, includes money and materials used to build factories, distribution centers, warehouses, or other infrastructure.

In our Snack Foods case, we reviewed the movement of AFG along the path from domestic to global focus. Though not all companies leave their home markets, those that do tend to follow the common path demonstrated by AFG. We now add some additional commentary on strategies for stages 2, 3, 4 and 5. These paths were first introduced in Chapter 6 but are reviewed again in Figure 38-1 below.

Figure 38-1

Stages on the Path of Globalization

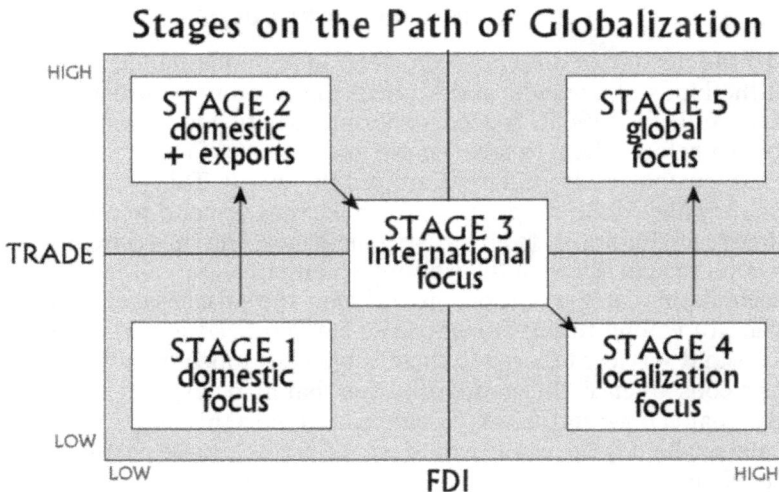

Stage 2: Domestic & Exporting

The movement to exporting is a natural and normal ambition for most domestic companies. Unless the product has a terrible weight-to-value ratio, such as bricks or cement, the savings captured through economies of scale often offset the shipping and other transaction costs associated with exporting. Often, a company's knowledge of and relationship with its existing suppliers and employees makes exporting an easy option. Bottom line: for many companies exports can cut per-unit costs and increase revenues at the same time, leading to higher overall profits.

Granted, some services are difficult to export. For example, if you are in the hotel business or legal profession and want to expand outside your home market, you will have a difficult time simply exporting your services. But even here, internet-based technologies have facilitated a range of creative export-oriented business models. For example, in 2011 global consumer spending on such things as media content and apps and services for mobile phones broke through the $100 billion barrier. It is difficult to know how much of this revenue involves cross-border sales, but most experts believe the number is significant and growing rapidly in these services. J.P. Morgan estimated that global e-commerce revenue alone was $963 billion in 2013. Beyond services, if you are making TVs, heavy machinery, cars, rice cookers, shoes, clothing, furniture, semiconductors, bulldozers, steel, cameras, copiers, or similar products, exporting is typically the first real move that companies make toward globalization. It is not surprising that world merchandise trade reached $18.3 trillion in 2012, a number that was about 10 percent larger than the entire U.S. economy.

Stage 3: International Focus

To the dismay of die-hard exporters, many potential customers demand the kinds of products and services that require a measure of local presence and adjustment. Indeed, exporters face two inconvenient truths that typically force them to take a more international focus.

First, customers are different around the world. They want different things, they have different price sensitivities, they prefer different packaging, they react differently to advertising messages, and they purchase what they want through different distribution channels.

Second, this category of consumers below the surface layer of customers who are willing to buy a company's standardized exports who want products and services tailored to them is typically much, much larger.

As a consequence, the standardization that made exports profitable is exactly what can get in the way of penetrating into this larger segment of customers, which is the essence of Stage 3. To reach these customers, you have to change many aspects of your products and services, as well as the way you distribute, market, sell, and provide customer service. The good news is that companies can often dramatically increase their revenues and total profits by adding local features and services and by altering the look and feel of products.

Even if you didn't want to reach this larger group of customers beyond those who readily accepted your standardized exports, export customers are often not the most loyal. Who can blame them? They complain about response times, warranties and repair work, and lack of advertising support. While in theory exporters can accommodate these concerns through hard work, the needs and worries of local customers are nearly impossible to address without some local presence.

As companies are pulled toward greater local investment in one country and then another, the strategic emphasis shifts away from exports and toward localization. Soon their operations include many different countries. Often a company with a strong international focus is one that embraces a regional approach to markets. Not surprisingly, there is considerable evidence suggesting that FDI is most frequently associated with regional strategies.

Complex regional strategies can involve multiple regions and often include numerous production capabilities within each region. However, because of the differences across regions, each region usually acts with a certain level of autonomy. General Motors, for example, in the 1990s had a distinct strategy and organization for Europe compared with North America. The same applied to companies like Caterpillar and Toshiba. Depending on the nature of the business, the differences among countries within a region can also be significant.

Regional strategies often make great sense for companies with a significant international footprint. It is hard to imagine a company with subsidiaries in 100 or more countries where each country office is completely independent and reports directly back to corporate headquarters. Regional organizations can be very helpful, and regional approaches may achieve operational efficiencies when the markets are large enough.

Finally, regional organizations provide the benefit of relatively clear lines of sight and accountabilities for senior leaders. To put it plainly, most managers can get their minds around a single region of the world, whether it is Latin America or Central Europe, whereas developing a global mindset can be much tougher. Developing a regional approach is not only more do-able but is often the best solution for companies with strong international ambitions.

Stage 4: Localization Focus

The pressures for localization do not stop as companies take on an international focus. The more companies internationalize, the more they replicate activities around the world. This adds significant costs. At the same time, customers continue to demand more localized services and features. Furthermore, pressures for just-in-time delivery of components or finished products put added pressure on companies to make and sell locally at a country level. Advances in production technologies also make lower scale assembly plants more cost-competitive than huge regional or global facilities. No wonder many companies move from an international focus to a straight localization focus. We see examples of this in the steel industry, where mini-mills are now often 30 percent more efficient than integrated mills. In other cases, government regulatory pressures, taxation, and trade barriers continue to favor local production, employment, sales, promotion, etc.

Whatever the reason, wide ranges of industries including food production, mining, specialty chemicals, and financial services have shifted
entire operations to a local country focus granting units a high degree of
local autonomy and enabling fast decision-making and customer responsiveness. In fact, the entire turnaround strategy for Carrefour, the second
largest retailer in the world, by its newly installed CEO in 2012 was to
move decision making and management down into the countries and even
to the level of store managers within countries.

It is important to note that companies that pursue high-localization
strategies can compete in just as many countries as companies with borderless global strategies. They can have similarly high levels of international sales as a percentage of total sales. However, often there are certain
activities that do not necessarily need to be different in every country and
the differences can add up to significant costs and inefficiencies. As a consequence, many high localization companies of the past, such as Kellogg,
Nestlé, Philips, and 3M, have now significantly revised their strategies and
moved toward the final stage of the globalization journey.

Stage 5: Global Focus

While Stage 4 gives companies great insights into difference customer
needs, regulations, supply chains, government relations, and the like,
Stage 5 is focused on determining what activities need to be different by
country or region and which ones can be globally integrated.

The need to move into Stage 5 is often not anticipated because the
downside of Stage 4 emerges slowly over time. Early in the process of
Stage 4, the total cost of the localization efforts is small. As the size of a
company's operations around the world grows, so too do the costs of doing
things differently in various countries. Like a lobster slowly brought to a
boil, you often don't notice the inefficiencies, redundancies, and duplications at first. Then finally, when they are large enough, you realize that the
costs of having lots of small factories, seventeen different finance systems,
and eleven different IT platforms are enormous. Yet these same redundancies, despite their costs, allow companies the added freedom to compete in
exciting new ways. How can companies best manage the tension between
being able to quickly serve local customer needs and the need to eliminate
unnecessary duplication and maximize global learning?

The transition into and the dynamics of borderless global competition
are marked by the reemergence of two dynamics that separately played
leading roles in earlier strategies. In the export stage, the economies of
scale and benefits of standardization pushed companies to focus on making something one way at home and then selling it largely the same way
around the world. In the international focus stage, the differences across
regions and countries pushed companies to begin to modify and adapt to
the local differences. In the borderless global stage both forces—the forces for global integration and for local adaptation—hold sway. As a conse-

quence, companies struggle with but eventually master a complex process of determining which things to globally integrate, which things to locally differentiate, and which activities and products should have unique blends of both.

To be certain, a borderless global strategy does not mean that companies do everything the same around the world. The common refrain to "think globally and act locally" is actually somewhat misguided. Why? Because as we observed in the Snack Foods story, borderless companies globally integrate and standardize in thought and action some things, while other things are locally differentiated in thought and action.

Companies with a truly global focus view their activities in totality, as if competitive battles were waged on a worldwide chessboard. The goal is global hegemony, which is often achieved by sacrificing profits or market position in one country for gains in another. Because they are fixated on the global scorecard, borderless global competitors lose their tight loyalty to their country of origin; they care more about worldwide market share, brand value, and competitiveness than about their success in a single market.

By thinking about the world in its entirety, global companies are better able to learn about best practices and are more capable of internalizing knowledge gained from wherever in the world it originates. They do this by rapidly and efficiently disseminating knowledge throughout their global operations. From their global vantage point, executives are best able determine appropriate resource allocations across countries and balance the emphasis on global integration and local responsiveness.

Paths Forward

There are always exceptions to the evolution of companies. As in most things in life, exceptions exist for every rule. This is certainly the case for companies that follow the globalization path. The preceding figure suggests a natural path forward for Stage 3 companies. Indeed, many use Stage 4 as a stepping stone to more complex global strategies as Stage 5 competitors. Others follow different paths forward. The two most common approaches include:

Option 1: Stay at Stage 3, international focus. Many successful companies—Ford Motor Company, Ernst & Young, and Novartis, to name just a few—have maintained a strong international focus for many years. Despite the appeal of having a global focus, in theory nothing forces companies to jump to Stage 5. In fact, the added complexity and difficulties faced by Stage 5 organizations often make this move dangerous and unnecessary. Well-run companies can prosper in all stages of their development. Progression from one stage to the next is neither necessary or inevitable.

Option 2: Skip Stage 4 entirely and move directly to the Stage 5, global focus. Companies such as Apple, Boeing, and Ferrari bypassed Stage 4 altogether in their march to the global focus of Stage 5.

Large international acquisitions are the quickest way of moving a company off a normal trajectory from domestic to exporting, from exporting to international focus, and so on. While it's strategically and financially risky, there are always examples of exceptional companies that jumped from domestic to global with one roll of the dice. Acquisition aside, in a few unique cases, e.g. Indian software service firms, it is also possible to find companies that leapfrog, skipping from exporting to borderless global strategies in one big leap. This is extremely rare. Rarer still are the examples of companies born as essentially borderless global competitors. These are typically fast-growing technology companies such as Skype and Google. When you dig deep into these examples, you invariably find a few years of domestic activity before the move to global.

Despite the exceptions, the model captures the path forward for the vast majority of firms today. As with any path, not all travelers make it from beginning to end. Most companies start and end their journeys as domestic companies. Fewer still make it through exporting to become internationally focused competitors. Rare are the examples of borderless global competitors. Yet given the huge benefits that come to companies that move along the path, we wonder why so few are able to successfully progress? Our answer comes in looking at the people side of the Failure to Globally Launch syndrome.

CHAPTER

39

THE PEOPLE SIDE

STRATEGIES WORK ONLY WHEN THE RIGHT PEOPLE ARE IN PLACE. NO MATTER the strategy, the right people are always those who have sufficient knowledge of the products and services sold by the company and the conditions under which they must work in order to succeed. As a consequence, leaders must have the requisite skills that correspond with each stage of the organizational side of the global way. The figure on the following page (Figure 39-1) captures the essence of the leadership imperatives of each stage on the global way.

Leaders have a lot of things to which they can pay *attention*. They can focus on different markets—for example, paying attention to what is happening in China, Germany, or Brazil. They can also focus their attention on what is happening at home. Attention is more proactive and encompassing than simple awareness. Leaders who attend to different markets are actively engaged in learning about and being mentally engaged with market, political, and competitive developments in particular geographies.

Separately, the *loyalty* of leaders can be centered on home customers and employees or on customers and employees from many countries. Loyalty implies putting the interests of one constituency ahead of another. Leaders who are loyal to their home country will put the interest of local customers ahead of the wants and needs of customers in a distant country. They will do this even when a more inclusive approach might maximize profits. Plus, with hiring and promotion decisions, leaders who are locally

Figure 39-1
The Global Way to Effective Leadership

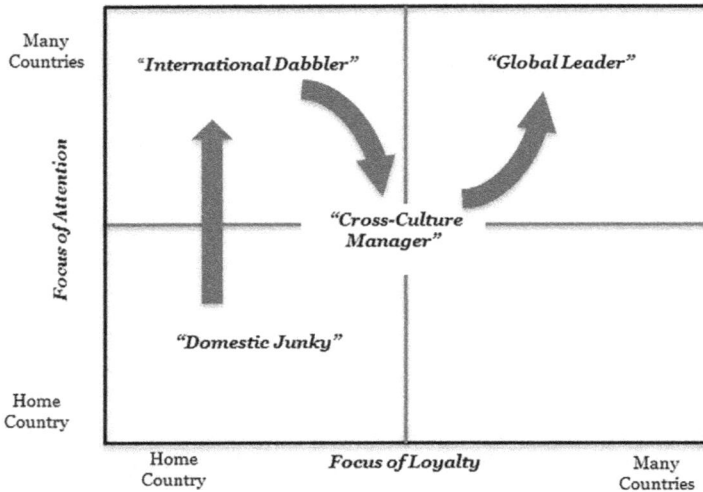

loyal are biased in favor of domestic employees. When layoffs are necessary, they would rather start with foreign employees and delay local layoffs to the bitter end.

Effective leaders closely align the focus of their attention and loyalties to their firm's strategy. The best leaders of domestic competitors are those whose focus is on what is happening at home. Because their companies are operating in only one country, they have no need to split their loyalties or balance the interests of domestic versus international stakeholders. Rather, their attention and commitments are centered on local suppliers, employees, and customers.

Domestic junkies are not particularly interested in what is happening outside their home countries; they are not distracted by events in far-off locations. They are often highly adept at connecting with local stakeholders and are skilled at tailoring products and service to meet local needs.

Finding domestic junkies is not difficult. The vast majority of business leaders in virtually every country are actually domestic junkies. They are the managers who are educated locally. They speak a single language and share an affinity for their home country's culture and values. They usually have not worked overseas lest their attention begin to shift to distant lands. Most are not aware of their home country bias. This is reinforced through their interactions with almost everyone they meet and with whom they work, including local unions and the bulk of white-collar workers. They are "junkies" because their domestic focus is deeply reinforced by their day-to-day experiences, friendships, and contacts. They live for their domestic life, and their habit of putting local first provides the reference for every major business decision they make. They become anxious and nervous when confronted by ideas and practices that are foreign to them.

Much of this is carried out at the sub-conscious level.

What is important to point out here is that domestically oriented leaders are not bad and are in fact good when the firm is also domestically focused. Problems occur when the firm needs to move to a new stage in its development. Major challenges occur when most senior leaders come out of its original stage (Domestic Focus) and have no experience in or orientation toward the next stages of development.

How this mismatch happens is easy to understand. For any firm that has had a history of being in Stage 1 for 20 years or more and for any firm based in a sizeable domestic market (US, Germany, France, Japan, UK, Spain, Brazil, Italy, etc.), it is easy for leaders to work their way to the top who have only had the opportunity to work at home. Both CEOs during David's tenure with the company had essentially zero international experience. While it is easy to understand how this mismatch happens, it doesn't lessen the challenges that the mismatch creates.

International Dabblers

In addition to the mismatch problem, domestic junkies are often unaware of new technologies and business models introduced overseas. Domestic junkies are easily blind-sided by new competitors that pop up seemingly unexpectedly. This is not such a big problem in industries that thrive on small mom-and-pop competitors, e.g. shoe repair shops, funeral homes, dentists, and the like. But for everyone else, leaders who are domestic junkies put their companies at serious risk because even if they are focused on their domestic market, that doesn't keep foreign firms from coming up with new and better technologies, products, processes, etc.

In contrast, international dabblers are more curious about foreign markets. Either they are keen to understand foreign market opportunities because of their hunger for growth, or they are just naturally curious about the world. In any case, their external focus means they are well suited for exporting strategies.

It is possible to turn domestic junkies into international dabblers, but it isn't easy. Some people focus attention on international markets because they have to. These folks become international dabblers because they are driven by business opportunities and feel compelled to focus their attention on new markets. In other cases, managers might have an unusually high level of natural curiosity about what is happening overseas. Maybe their interest has been sparked by overseas travel, or maybe they were born with unexplained wanderlust. In either case, business-charged or natural interest, curiosity is only partially open to influence.

While international dabblers search for new markets for their company's products and services, their hearts remain largely at home. Because their loyalties are centered in their home country, they are biased in favor of local ideas and practices. They find it difficult to let go and embrace products, people, or practices from other parts of the world. The home country experiences that have guided them throughout their lives prevent them from moving far outside their domestic comfort zones.

While international dabblers are far fewer in number than domestic junkies, the transition to a more export-centered dabbler mindset comes quite naturally for a sub-set of people. It represents a shift in thinking, but rarely does it challenge the core identity of the leader.

Cross-Culture Manager

At the minimum these people are great at working across their home culture to one other country, often because they lived and worked in the second country. An example would be an American who worked and lived in Korea or China for extended periods of time. At the other end of the continuum would be people who are experts at doing business in multiple countries within a given region. For example, they might be quite knowledgeable about and comfortable with working in Latin America. They may even speak both Portuguese and Spanish. Or they may be quite knowledgeable about and comfortable with working in Western Europe. They may speak French, Spanish, and Italian—facilitated by the common romance language base. They exhibit a breadth of skills at understanding a wide array of customers. Most important, they possess the mental acumen to make sense of often competing demands while at the same time deriving common approaches to generalizable problems.

The good news for cross-culture managers is their geographic span of attention is actually less than what is required for either successful international dabblers or global leaders. The scope of their world has been pre-determined by the company, and the domain of company politics has been largely fixed within the region. When their geographic territory is Europe, for example, they don't need to worry about what is happening in Asia or North America—at least not much.

Creating cross-culture managers is never easy. Finding people with the ability to understand another country and culture, let alone several in a region is one problem. Shifting their loyalty can be even more difficult. This is particularly true as the distance grows between the manager's home country and the cultural norms of other countries in the region. For example, an American manager will have a much easier time transitioning to a regional North American role than to a regional role in Asia Pacific. Bottom line: creating cross-cultural managers is far less challenging if the managers remain in their home region.

The loyalty challenge is a tough nut to crack. Why is it so difficult? Because almost every manager is naturally biased in favor of leadership models and approaches learned at home. Even if they embraced a broader perspective of loyalty, their natural approach to leadership is often sub-optimal within their assigned region. For this reason, the transition from international dabbler to cross-culture manager is tough, and the path is littered with disappointment. This is in part why an important percentage of people sent on their very first expatriate assignment fail to adjust to the new country and culture.[2]

Even when the match between the person and the leadership need is strong, not all cross-culture managers find fulfilling careers. Because of their regional backgrounds, cross-cultural managers often have somewhat limited career opportunities for promotion at corporate head office. This reality, plus the potential to be misunderstood or under-appreciated by head office, means that the best-in-breed cross-cultural managers often prefer working for regional companies and not the regional offices of multinational companies. After all, why work for a global MNC where your skills will be under-appreciated, you will face prejudice, and you will have more limited career opportunities?

Global Leaders.

By far the toughest of all leadership positions is that of the global leader. Global leaders are loyal to all customers and employees, regardless of country affiliation. To make their jobs even more difficult, they pay attention to multiple markets. They do this not sequentially—for example, focusing first on Japan, then the next day on China, then on Germany—but concurrently.[3] They have the mental acuity to focus on the entire world with competing interests and often confusing data that requires enormous mental focus.[4] Global leaders are successful because they overcome national differences and embrace best practices from around the world.

Global leaders possess a range of skills including customer centricity, strategic acumen, and organizational and business savvy. They are able to recognize market opportunities that others would miss. These include arbitrage opportunities involving cost and quality difference across countries, new market opportunities for the company's goods and services, and efficiency-maximizing opportunities that come through global economies of scale and redundancy reductions through standardization. To pull this off, global leaders understand the product lines offered by key subsidiaries, the cost structures and overall competitiveness of key subsidiaries, the location and quality of technological resources (both hard assets and people) within the global organization, and the location of managerial and employee talent within the global organization.

Global leaders don't just need global business skills, they also need the ability to connect with people—customers, suppliers, thought leaders, and employees—from incredibly diverse backgrounds and cultural orientations. Plus they need to do this without prejudice or even giving the appearance of bias. None of this is easy.

Not surprisingly, global leaders are few and far between in the world today. Most companies are begging for more of them. Why are they in such short supply? Because creating global leaders is uniquely challenging.

The most natural way forward is to turn cross-culture managers into global leaders. After all, they have already shown multicultural skills and have made moves to broaden their loyalties. However, the skills and attitudes of global leaders are fundamentally different from and more sophisticated than cross-culture managers. There is a world of difference between a skilled European or Asia Pacific manager and a true global leader. The competencies, loyalties, and attention focus of global leaders are distinct.

CHAPTER

40

CIRCUMVENTING THE GLOBAL FAILURE TO LAUNCH

THE PATH TO BECOMING A BORDERLESS GLOBAL COMPETITOR IS DIFFICULT and not suitable for all companies. While not every company can or even should have global ambitions, those that do often fall short of reaching their goals. Those that try and fail are inevitably surprised because they have little experience with major international disappointments. The path they have traveled might have had a few bumps, but for most the journey has been ongoing and directionally forward for decades.

The failure to globally launch inevitably happens as the company moves its focus from international to borderless global. Most often the failure stems from leadership shortcomings. Leadership that lags strategy is leadership that fails. Remember the spacecraft analogy we shared earlier? Just as a spacecraft must fire its booster rockets well before reaching the outer limits of the atmosphere, so must companies fire the equivalent of their leadership development rockets well *before* they shift their strategy from international to global. Failure to do so will result in a failure to globally launch.

Companies need to take specific steps to groom leaders at every stage of their development. Creating global leaders requires unique steps that don't come naturally for companies or for most candidates for the role. From our experience, we have identified ten critical actions that will help accelerate the process and ensure successful global launches:

1. Create unique global leader competency models, so all managers know what *good* looks like.
2. Prepare succession plans that move people into and out of cross-culture manager roles. The number of people in these roles needs to be meaningful so their impact is broadly and deeply felt throughout the organization.
3. Build global leadership learning academies to accelerate the development of global skills.
4. Introduce a new category of global leaders in company organization charts. These leaders should be given clearly delineated global responsibilities, accountabilities, and job titles.
5. Embrace more robust assessment models that consider global leadership skills and acumen.
6. Create best practice forums that introduce leading edge ideas (from inside and outside the firm) to the global organization. Ensure that global leaders play a role *teaching* and showcasing these practices.
7. Revise compensation schemes to promote behaviors that encourage managers to broaden their interests to include the global fortunes of the firm. Key to this are efforts to shift the loyalty of senior managers to global customers, employees, and suppliers.
8. Review overall corporate culture to separate values and behaviors that are globally applicable from those that are (and should remain) country-specific. Clearly identify those values and behaviors that are universal, and ensure that they are communicated and reinforced.
9. Hire and promote non-natives of the home country into senior leadership positions at head office. This will not only signal to the rest of the organization that cross-cultural skills are important, but will also strengthen the DNA mix of the senior leadership team.
10. Consider moving from head office certain functional activities, divisions, or units to different countries when the home country's business environment stifles global dialogue and restricts recruiting and retention of the best talent.

None of these steps is easy. Nor can they be taken without the full support of the CEO and board. They require humility, perseverance, and a team effort. Table 40-1 summarizes the key attributes of leaders at each step along the way.

Table 40-1
Key Leadership Attributes along the Global Way

	Focus of Attention	Loyalty of Leaders	Key International Skills	How they are created
Domestic Junkies	Local/within home country	Local, centered on home country	N/A	Home bred and grown
International Dabblers	Mostly domestic but also on multiple international markets	Centered on the home country	Scanning countries for market opportunities	Often self-chosen from ranks of Domestic Junkies
Cross-Culture Managers	One region of the world	Multiple countries within the region	Connecting with regional stakeholders Driving regional efficiencies Culture and language specific to region	Hired overseas
Global Leaders	Global, concurrent attention focused on all key markets	All major and potential markets	Global scanning Prioritizing market opportunities Globally integrating operations	Advanced through ranks of Continental Champions Accelerated development through effective succession planning

The Global Way

The path to global leadership is difficult and dangerous. Companies can and do stumble. Too often leaders make the mistake of believing that past success is the best predictor of future glory. Yet those who have been successful leading one type of organization are often not the best at leading another type of organization. Blasting into orbit requires a conscious effort to build leaders who are ideally suited for the *next* stage of growth, not the current one. Unfortunately, companies are usually lousy at the task and often fail in the process. The sad truth is that global leaders are often best at developing themselves, and they prosper despite the prevailing norms of their companies.

The imperatives of globalization are primarily economic. To achieve these gains, humans struggle to overcome biases in loyalty and frailties in their attentional abilities. They battle their own weaknesses and struggle to cope with and ultimately overcome the frailties of their co-workers. By acknowledging these weaknesses and compensating for them through proactive leadership development processes, the *Global Way* can be a rewarding path for all to take.

ENDNOTES

1   Dunning, J. "Globalization and the theory of MNE activity." In N. Hood and S. Young (eds), *The Globalization of Multinational Enterprise*. London: Macmillan, 1999. See also, Toyne, B., and Nigh, D. *International Business: An Emerging View*. Columbia, SC: University of South Carolina Press, 1997.

2   Black, J. Stewart, Hal B. Gregersen, Mark E. Mendenhall, and Linda Stroh. (1999) *Globalizing People Through International Assignments*, Reading, Mass.: Addison-Wesley.

ABOUT THE AUTHORS

Allen Morrison, Ph.D.

ALLEN MORRISON IS A PROFESSOR OF GLOBAL MANAGEMENT AND THE HOLD-er of the Kristian Gerhard Jebsen Chair of Responsible Leadership at IMD, based in Lausanne Switzerland. Allen is also the Director of IMD's Global CEO Center, which focuses on the challenges CEOs face while leading their companies in the global economy. Allen has authored or co-authored over 60 articles and case studies, and ten books. His research has been published in a range of journals including *Strategic Management Journal, Sloan Management Review, Journal of Management*, the *Journal of International Business Studies* and the *Harvard Business Review*.

Prior to joining IMD, Dr. Morrison was on the faculty at INSEAD where he also served as Director of executive development for INSEAD North America. Allen was also a tenured full professor and held the Bombardier Chair of Global Management at the Ivey Business School at the University of Western Ontario. At the Ivey Business School, Allen served as Associate Dean of Executive Development. Dr. Morrison has been a visiting professor at both the Anderson School at UCLA and CEIBS in China.

Executive leadership—particularly the development of global executives—is the primary focus on Morrison's work. Professor Morrison conducts executive seminars and consults with a wide range of companies around the world. Global strategy, global leadership development, and responsible leadership are key themes in the workshops, seminars and speeches delivered by Morrison.

Dr. Morrison received his undergraduate degree in international relations from Brigham Young University and his MBA from the Ivey Business School at the University of Western Ontario. He received his Ph.D. in international business strategy from the Darla Moore School, University of South Carolina.

J. Stewart Black, Ph.D.

DR. BLACK IS PROFESSOR OF GLOBAL LEADERSHIP AND STRATEGY AT IMD. HE specializes in leadership, strategy, change, globalization, and stakeholder engagement.

Dr. Black has worked with a variety of for-profit and non-profit organizations in all major regions of the world, but has spent nearly half his career living and working in Asia. Specifically, Dr. Black has conducted numerous top management retreats working with senior teams to analyze their environment, formulate strategy, and align organizational and leadership capabilities to achieve business objectives. These engagements have involved process skills in getting the team through discussions and debates to points of decision and commitment, as well as content knowledge in key areas such as strategy, change, and human resources.

Dr. Black is a leading instructor and scholar in leadership, strategy, change management, globalization, and human capital. He is the author or co-author of 15 books. These included highly acclaimed textbooks used at various universities around the world, such as *Management: Meeting New Challenges, Organizational Behavior, International Business Environments: Text and Cases*, and books written specifically for managers, such as It *Starts with One: Changing Individuals Changes Organizations, The Global Leadership Challenge, Sunset in the Land of the Rising Sun, International Assignments: An Integration of Research and Practice, Globalizing People through International Assignments*, and So *You Are Going Overseas: A Handbook for Personal and Professional Success.*

Dr. Black is the author of over 80 articles and cases in both managerial and academic publications: *Business Week, The Wall Street Journal, Fortune, Workforce, International Business, Mobility, Personnel, Academy of Management Review, Academy of Management Journal, Human Resource Management, Group & Organization Studies, International Journal of Intercultural Relations, Asia-Pacific Journal of Management, Journal of International Business Studies*, and *Human Relations.*

Dr. Black received his undergraduate degree in psychology and English from Brigham Young University, where he graduated with honors. He earned his master degree from the business school at Brigham Young University, where he was on the dean's list and graduated with distinction. After graduation, he worked for a Japanese consulting firm, where he eventually held the position of managing director. Dr. Black returned to the U.S. and received his Ph.D. in Business Administration from the University of California, Irvine.

Dr. Black started his career on the faculty at the Amos Tuck School of Business Administration, Dartmouth College. Later he was a professor of business administration at the University of Michigan and Executive Director of the school's Asia Pacific Human Resource Partnership. Prior to joining IMD, Dr. Black was an Associate Dean for Executive Development Programs and Professor of Management Practice in Global Leadership and Strategy at INSEAD.

www.ingramcontent.com/pod-product-compliance
Lightning Source LLC
Chambersburg PA
CBHW031938190326
41519CB00007B/583